ARTWORK
Peter Campbell

ARTWORK
Peter Campbell

London Review
OF BOOKS

P

PROFILE BOOKS

First published in Great Britain in 2012 by
PROFILE BOOKS LTD
3A Exmouth House
Pine Street
London ECIR OJH
www.profilebooks.com

Published in association with the
London Review of Books
28 Little Russell Street
London WC1A 2HN
www.lrb.co.uk

10 9 8 7 6 5 4 3 2 1

Design by James Alexander/Jade Design
Printed and bound in Italy by Graphicom

A CIP catalogue record for this book is available from
the British Library.

ISBN 978 1 78 125067 9
eISBN 978 1 84 765910 1

Foreword
Bill Manhire

PETER CAMPBELL'S father signed my School Certificate. And my wife Marion's. Indeed he did the same for everyone we knew. Peter's father had been New Zealand's director general of education. But about Peter himself there was nothing remotely stern or headmasterly, although he could sometimes look at you over his glasses in a mildly quizzical way.

We coincided in various places – Menton and Martinborough, Wellington and London – but then New Zealanders are always coming and going. The current diaspora is said to be about one million – one-fifth of the population. Back in the 1960s Peter and Win had exchanged the hills of Wellington – the little wooden capital with its wind and water and sometimes vertical terrain – for life in London. They were probably members of the last generation of New Zealanders who travelled to Europe by ship, who perhaps felt they had to decide whether or not to stay away. Now young New Zealanders do their OE (Overseas Experience), and come home and settle down, much like medieval Icelanders who went a-viking; or in some cases stay away simply as a lifestyle option that can be reformulated according to need. They chat on Facebook; they tweet.

There are always a few people you feel extraordinarily close to, even though you don't often meet face to face or correspond much; as Peter once remarked, the quality of a friendship can be quite disproportionate to the hours you spend together. Talking was one of the very best things about Peter whenever there was some time. Occasionally he and Win would lend us their little Judd Street flat, high up among the chimney pots of Bloomsbury, with a Mary Poppins view through to the roofline of St Pancras. Peter would arrive at about 8.30 each morning, having walked the mile and a half or so from Embankment tube station, and then we might talk for an hour before he settled down to work and we went out for the day.

The talk would be about family and friends, but it was always interlaced with news of what he was reading. Peter had an astonishing range of things he was reading, had read, had in mind to read, was about to reread. Lucky for him, he made a living outside the academy; his personal taste was not subject to fixed or fashionable curricula, or to research projects driven by revenue needs. Perhaps that is why his talk was always lucid yet asymmetrical, full of human drift. As in his LRB columns, he made things vivid without raising his voice. He could pass from Elizabeth Bishop to Carl Hiassen to Georgette Heyer without blinking an eye, without any sense that he was going from high to low or that he was taking part in some cultural studies display. You needed to know some arcane things to bat the ball back to him. I could talk about Denis Glover, the New Zealand poet and printer from whom he had first learned about typography; and I could offer Camille Flammarion and Sir John Herschel (both of whom I was reading for poetic fodder) or Dennis Wheatley, whose *The Man Who Missed the War* I had been reading in a not very successful attempt to survey the whole field of fiction about Antarctica. But Peter knew far more about Dennis Wheatley than I did, and he could always go on to suggest Eric Ambler or the sad case of Joe Gould, about both of whom I was ignorant. It sounds competitive, but it wasn't. Sharing books, and the prospect of books, was one of his forms of friendship.

The Campbell hospitality would continue in even richer ways around the kitchen table at the house in Gartmoor Gardens, Southfields, where Win and Peter settled in 1963, a short walk from Wimbledon. A couple of times we visited them there while the tennis was on: you stepped out of the tube onto a platform decked out in artificial lawn with dinky white lines. This delighted us, but I think made Peter shrug and sigh a little. He mentions Wimbledon in an LRB piece of 2004, 'In the Park'. There are tides of tennis fans who must be elbowed through, plus the sacrifice of Wimbledon Park for a fortnight to fans' parking needs, which leads him, via the park's changing wildlife, to its changing human population – namely, the influx of young Australians and South Africans. 'The invaders are less colourful, but in their way just as exotic as the new geese and ducks. Like the birds they bring their problems. The geese leave droppings on the grass; the antipodean mini-barbecues leave burnt patches. They tend to party noisily. But I came from New Zealand: who am I to complain?'

That column then goes on to consider other London parks, and the places of retreat and recreation they have become for exiles and emigrants; and then somehow he is in the world of urban stucco, and soon enough he is talking about Nash, who 'began the democratisation of grandeur', and half-imagining (then pulling quietly back) what Nash might have done if called on to design a shopping mall. (Peter's what-ifs were always interesting: 'I would like to see a modern Temple of Janus, its

doors closed only in times of peace, on the empty plinth in Trafalgar Square.')

His discourse on parks makes its way forward very like one of his walks, or the way he talked. You would start somewhere, with a destination in mind, but movement itself was important and distractions always possible. At..., the book of Peter's LRB contributions, begins with a walk around the area just north of King's Cross, along St Pancras Road – 'in a pause between dereliction and transformation'. That prolonged, hesitating moment, where movement and change have just occurred but also loom, seems typical of him, and there is something of that in his cover images for the LRB. The sightlines can be slightly unusual. The images always seem animated, or about to become so: they don't freeze what they see.

Peter knew first-hand what the word 'kinetic' meant. One of his earliest memories was of an earthquake: 'The whole house was in motion,' he wrote in the LRB. 'We moved with it.' This, along with his tramping experiences on New Zealand's swing bridges, prepared him (perhaps more than any engineering and architectural knowledge) to think about the wobble in the Millennium Bridge. 'Reading about it I felt it in my feet.'

As far as New Zealandness goes, his skills of self-efface-ment and understatement would have been well developed long before he got to London. But he practised them there. Whenever he talked about the LRB, it was with a sense of great good fortune. He could make himself sound peripheral to the whole enterprise – someone who, you know, helped out a bit – without making the magazine seem anything less than central to his life.

'Something nasty seems to be going on,' was one of his more chilling understatements. His illness must have been very hard to bear. I'm told he continued to read, and to reread, but he must have felt he was reading against the clock. He must have relearned the heaviness of books, even as he learned new words like 'oramorph'. Kim was his very last book – one of the rereads.

'The expatriate condition is complicated,' he said to me once in an email. 'You transplant yourself, but bring a lot of native soil on your roots.' In his last days, he had some satisfaction from that complication. He was at home in Southfields, but one of his nurses was from Tauranga. 'The sweetest nurse,' Win wrote later to say. 'She would lean over him to moisten his mouth and talk to him in the familiar accent of his youth. She looks like a dark beauty from an old master painting and I can't but believe that he greatly appreciated that and that she improved his final hours.'

Encounters with Peter didn't only take place in London. There was also Wellington, which he visited several times in the last dozen years, and which offered natives like us the opportunity to boast about the local coffee. Or we would see him with our mutual friends Chris and Margaret Cochran in Martinborough, a small country town set among wineries, where the streets – Venice, New York, Panama – are named after places the settle-ment's founder once visited, and where the central square and its converging streets are laid out in the shape of the Union Jack.

There was also Menton, where Marion and I lived for some months in 2004, and where Peter and Win came to stay with us. We sat on the balcony of the Palais Lutetia, admiring the town's parking problems, and talked. We walked on the sea-front. We went up to Sainte-Agnès and ate well. And we made a cemetery expedition. If we had been true rugby-loving New Zealanders, the grave of William Webb Ellis would have been our destination (there is a rue W. Webb Ellis adjoining the rue Katherine Mansfield). But instead we went in search of Aubrey Beardsley, one of many young tuberculosis sufferers who are buried in Menton. I had a camera; Peter had binoculars. It took several hours in the Mediterranean heat, perhaps because it was an impulse quest, rather than anything planned, but also because we started in the wrong cemetery – the one that sits just above the old town – before we eventually made our way to the Cimetière du Trabuquet, further up the hill. And there, after all, was a rather plain, disappointing grave – just a slab with a cross on it – but with a good sea view. We had expected an extravagant grotto. Still, the journey rather than the arrival matters: we were pleased with ourselves. Later I sent photos. They were full of vistas, and in some of them glasses of wine were being raised. Peter emailed back, with thanks. 'We may not look pretty,' he said, 'but don't we look happy!'

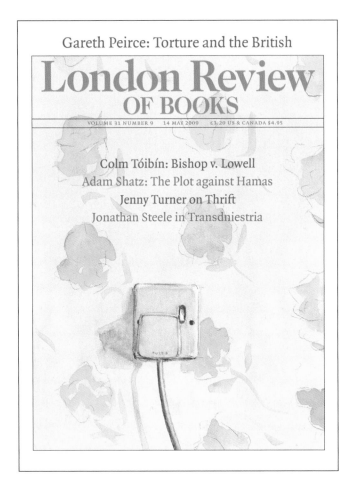

Gareth Peirce: Torture and the British

London Review
OF BOOKS

VOLUME 31 NUMBER 9   14 MAY 2009   £3.20 US & CANADA $4.95

Colm Tóibín: Bishop v. Lowell
Adam Shatz: The Plot against Hamas
Jenny Turner on Thrift
Jonathan Steele in Transdniestria

Hilary Mantel: The Virgin and I

London Review
OF BOOKS

VOLUME 31 NUMBER 7   9 APRIL 2009   £3.20 US & CANADA $4.95

Michael Wood: G.K. Chesterton
Graham Usher: India in Afghanistan
Marina Warner: Dear Old Khayyám   Rosemary Hill: Bowen in Love
J. Hoberman: Red Chagall   Christopher Clark: Nazi Toffs

Alan Bennett's Review of the Year

London Review
OF BOOKS

VOLUME 23 NUMBER 2   25 JANUARY 2001   £2.95 US & CANADA $5.95

David Trotter:
Wyndham Lewis

Lorna Sage:
Henry Green

Andrew O'Hagan:
A Story

Malcolm Bull:
Judas Saves

Glen Newey:
Chomsky

Andy Beckett
in Santiago

Conor Gearty:
Watch the
Judges

NEAL ASCHERSON: The Scottish Empire

London Review
OF BOOKS

VOLUME 33 NUMBER 19   6 OCTOBER 2011   £3.20 US & CANADA $4.95

DANIEL SOAR: You can't get away from Google
JAMES WOOD on Sebald's 'Austerlitz'
ANDREW O'HAGAN: Tweeting at an Execution
COLIN BURROW: Extreme Editing

Introduction
Jeremy Harding

PETER CAMPBELL'S illustrations appeared on more than four hundred covers of the *London Review of Books*. Most of these works are watercolours, with only a handful of pieces in other media, including collage, photography, pastel, oil and gouache. A few were computer-generated. Peter was involved with the *LRB* at the outset: his was the original design for the paper in 1979, and he steered it through a further two makeovers. In the early years, it was Peter who looked after the covers. Sometimes he commissioned photographs or went out and took them himself, but mostly he selected work from picture libraries and agency stock. Then in 1993 the designer became the cover artist.

This book, with its selection of finished covers, gives a good sense of Peter's skills as a colourist and draughtsman, his feeling for landscape and still life, his affection for what was in front of him or in his mind's eye.* It confirms the kinds of attention he paid to the world outside the window, the room he'd just entered, or the things he liked and went on to arrange on a table. Papers, fruit, typewriters, flowers in a porcelain jug. And of course it shows the energetic play of his intelligence once he brought it to bear on a pattern or framing motif, for example, or a brisk, formal study in which one shape has assented to the presence of another, or a graceful, low-key lesson in the properties of colour.

Then there are his people. People about in the great outdoors, often a bit retro, in cars, on bikes – Peter liked bicycles – or waiting on railway platforms: destination is a favourite theme. Leisure is another: idlers, sunbathers, deckchair habitués. Coming indoors, he liked to drape a man over an armchair or sit a young woman on a bed with her back to us. Inside and out, he enjoyed figures in well-defined roles: jockeys, trainers and lads; butlers, waiters and maître d's; dancers and players, tenors and tumblers, tailors' dummies.

Peter also had a sub-style which, without being abstract in the strict sense, catches the drift of abstract painting and places it at the service of a magazine cover. Sometimes he would take a device that might have been repeated successfully as a decorative surround and let it loose in its own right, like a Miró asterisk, looking on with avuncular interest to see how it coped with its new independence. Covers in this mode contained curious forms – chevrons, calligraphic twirls, characters from an imaginary font – acclimatising nicely to the pale colour washes where he set them down. Then there were emptier, altogether larger 'abstracts' suggestive of desert and steppe, where bands of colour were laid down rapidly on wet paper, one after the other, the edge of one band bleeding here and there into its predecessor. At times the darkest, thinnest band would hint deliberately at a horizon; at others it abandoned its pretensions and settled back as matter on the picture plane.

The unselfconsciousness and ease with which Peter moved between these idioms also took him fluently from one painterly reference to the next: his head was populated with the works of masters, classical and modern, and had been since his years as a teenager in New Zealand, where he was born in 1937. Often he alludes to the painters he happened to be thinking about at the time he was doing a cover. Many of his male subjects might have come to the *LRB* down a corridor hung with sketches by Daumier and Ardizzone. One of his afternoon-tea-scapes, with a picnic waiting under a parasol, pays obvious tribute to Eric Ravilious. A fiddle and bow rehearse an air from Dufy. A wild stretch of highland (dabs of ochre and weals of black) restages the panache of Ivon Hitchens; the upper part of the landscape is raised on a sheer flank of pink and pale blue: pure Peter Campbell.

A cover from 1996 depicts a multicoloured chequerboard, nine cells by nine, with a dozen or more reserved areas, and reminds us obliquely of Paul Klee's grids. A few years later, in 2002, Peter designed the exhibition catalogue for *Paul Klee: The Nature of Creation* at the Hayward. Walking readers around the show in a piece for the *LRB*, he singled out the watercolour backgrounds of Klee's oil-transfer drawings for special attention. 'There is no twentieth-century artist of equal importance,' he wrote, 'who depended so much on paper and transparency.'

In Peter's own grid for the *LRB* there are twenty-five square cells: the rest are narrow rectangles, separating the squares like buffers. Two thin lines intersecting at ninety degrees divide the entire design into four parts. Each of the parts contains four, six or nine of the master cells. This arrangement caused Peter a good deal of private enjoyment and though he spoke about it at the time, no one remembers precisely why. Perhaps there's a clue in the fact that 2:3, the golden ratio, was the proportion favoured in the design of medieval manuscripts, a theory

Perry Anderson: Italy's Decline

London Review
OF BOOKS

VOLUME 31 NUMBER 4 · 26 FEBRUARY 2009 · £3.20 US & CANADA $4.95

Michael Wood: Amira Hass:
The Part about Bolaño   After Gaza

Eric Hobsbawm: Steve Fraser:
Mandarin Science   Emma Goldman

Gilberto Perez: David Kaiser:
Time and Tarkovsky   Paul Dirac

advanced by Jan Tschichold, the designer and typographer who brought the first illustrations to Penguin covers in the 1940s. Before and during his time with the LRB, Peter was a book designer. He would have enjoyed the challenge of transposing the 2:3 ratio, *sotto voce*, to a colourful patchwork of cells.

Finally, the exercise reminds us of another in *The Elements of Drawing*. Ruskin's advice to students in Letter I, Exercise VII was to draw a grid on Bristol board and paint alternate squares, repeating the process until they could 'strike the colour up to the limit with perfect accuracy'. By practising on grid after grid, like a series of chessboards, the novice would learn to stop the pigment ponding at the bottom of each square. He called it 'leading a colour down'. Peter was no good at chessboards – a reader once wrote in to complain that he'd put a black square in the right-hand corner on a cover – but he knew how to lead a colour down, creating a uniform field, and he also became a great exponent of the graded wash, progressively adding water so that the pigment appeared to ebb as the brush went on its way. Like the wealth of reference he brought to his pictures, the suggestion of technical skill was underplayed in his finished pieces.

It's odd, given his versatility and his many acts of homage, oblique or obvious, that there's such a thing as a Peter Campbell. But there is and it's hard to mistake. Some of the best signature work is without decoration or abstraction and has no human figures: the convivial still lifes, the beguiling landscapes and subdued yet stagey interiors (an empty palm court, an unadorned corridor, a room with the tousled contents of a suitcase on the bed).

But signature was seldom the primary consideration: the purpose of a cover was to extend some form of welcome to the world. Neither vain nor especially modest, Peter understood that the good host doesn't make too much of himself. Hospitality, as far as a paper is concerned, is not just about readers: there are the contributors to think of as well. The charm of Peter's work appeals to the reader, and the world, but there is also a structural courtesy reserved for contributors. In many of his compositions he left plenty of neutral space where the names of writers and their stated business could be advertised: 'Hilary Mantel on Doris Lessing'; 'Frank Kermode: How Jesus got his face', 'James Wood: From a Novel in Progress', 'John Ashbery: "In the Village of Sleep"', and so on. Working around the contributors

and their stories was something Peter got used to. It must have been like turning down a bed in a hotel room before the celebrity arrived.

That's where his manservants and restaurant staff, also a bit retro, come in. 'Peter's flunkies', as we used to think of them, were there to announce that everything in an issue was as it should be. They were cheerful personifications of his own duties as designer and cover artist. Peter could create a mood of anticipation just as well with the lights on a Christmas tree or the head waiter standing in an empty dining room. But if he suspected this wasn't enough to entice readers into the paper's austere interiors, with the plain four-column format he'd designed, he might decide to take things up a notch and evoke the thrill of the show. Just as you'd got used to his decorative fancies or his quick, confident landscapes, you were confronted by an acrobat halfway across a wire, or a gnome-like actor bowing stage right.

Performance could also solve the problem of presenting words on a cover. The void he'd left for writers and their subjects would be dressed in a range of ingenious ways, as a bare stage drop, a movie screen, a lecture platform, a canvas on an artist's easel, a still photographer's studio, or any number of exotic entrances to tents, seraglios, marquees. The same ceremonial vacuum could also become an open book with no text, an unfurled scroll, or an oblong box with pretty packaging folded back on four sides. The basic themes – giving and taking, touting for business and catching the act, showing off and being at the show – allowed him to create a sense of occasion from a routine technical constraint.

But Peter the facilitator could sometimes put his foot down. Plenty of his drafts offered stiff resistance to the words. In a piece about him after his death, Mary-Kay Wilmers, the editor of the LRB, wrote that 'there was an unstated war between covers that couldn't accommodate words and covers that were all words – as sometimes they had to be.' Peter would bring in work that defied the editorial staff to put anything on it at all, and quite often this was how it appeared, pristine, with no more information than the masthead and a single story on the strapline. The sweeping interior of a terraced house, viewed through the sash window at the front, was published in 1998 under the strapline 'Seven Essays for a Rainy Summer'. (A slim

HUGH ROBERTS: Who said Gaddafi had to go?

London Review
OF BOOKS

VOLUME 35 NUMBER 22 17 NOVEMBER 2013 £3.20 US & CANADA $4.95

young woman is carrying a tray of tea things left to right.) The following summer, not so wet, a London garden in full leaf, viewed from the house, appeared beneath the rubric 'Big June Issue!' So much for words. The last picture he did for a cover before his death in October 2011 – a Wimbledon townscape with a fox moving smartly down the road – had allowed space for a couple of lines of text above or around its jaunty protagonist, but it appeared intact, slightly eerie, under a strapline about Libya.

Pictures weren't commissioned according to the likely contents of a coming issue: the LRB is not so seamlessly run and the world, across the space of a fortnight, not that easy to predict. Covers were chosen on the Thursday of each press week from a stock of paintings in the office which Peter would replenish with one or two new works every month. In her valedictory piece Wilmers wrote about the process of deciding on a picture:

> The considerations were simple: season (no beaches in winter, no bare trees in summer); general appropriateness (no ice-cream sundaes in wartime); and how many pieces had to be signalled on the cover. Sometimes a cover would hang around for a year and suddenly find favour ... The only literal connection I remember between a cover and the content was in an issue with a piece by Jenny Diski that eventually became her book *Skating to Antarctica*: Peter did a wonderful painting of the moon in its successive movements, rising and falling over a polar landscape. That may have been a pure coincidence (nobody can remember) and in any case the piece advertised on the rubric – it was the first issue of 1997 – was Alan Bennett's 'What I did in 1996.' One thing Bennett didn't do was skate to Antarctica.

WATERCOLOUR suited Peter, and his sense of how his time was best spent. His brief was to look things up and down and then record what he had seen and how it came to appear the way it did. His extraordinary pieces for the LRB about the round of exhibitions, the great collections, and the changing face of London, are all about looking and divulging. Much of his working life was spent prowling the galleries and glossing the metropolis for his readers in these discursive biweekly bulletins.

Toward the end of Peter's life his friend Robin Kinross published a selection in *At... writing from the 'London Review of Books'*. He had filed nearly three hundred pieces by then: the editors

kept him busy. In the course of Peter's day there was often a lot to see but not much time to record. Sometimes his decisions, which can seem beautifully judged in retrospect, were taken at quite a lick. This is true of the covers as well as the writing.

As far as the covers are concerned, watercolour got him where he wanted to go at just the right tempo, ensuring that the portfolio in the office was regularly resupplied. Among his books, he kept a copy of C. J. Holmes's lectures on the 'science of picture-making', first published in 1909. It's in a passage from Holmes – an artist as well as an art historian – that we come closest to the merits of watercolour as they must have seemed to Peter: 'It is simple and rapid in manipulation, it renders delicate tones with ease ... no other process is so rich in felicitous accident, so crisp and fresh in character.' (Or in its low-tech way, more admirably suited to the requirements of journalism. Watercolour, Holmes added with a raised eyebrow, was also 'pre-eminently the medium of tricks and dodges'.) Peter might complete a cover in a day or so, give or take the final touches, sometimes less. Summer seemed to bring on more labour-intensive studies – lavish picnic baskets and layered greenery done with a succession of glazes – but more often he liked to move along at a rate, painting wet on wet, pacing his performance against the speed at which his paper dried, charging areas of the picture with colour, lifting pigment off others, leaving little embankments of bleeding to stand.

Peter worked in the front room of the family home in Southfields, and a bare-bones studio in a flat in King's Cross. He kept a stock of good loose leaf paper and watercolour block, the leaves gummed down on three sides to prevent curling and puckering. He liked 100 per cent cotton blocks, fine grained, to take his drybrush detail, cold-pressed for maximum absorbency. His most delicate washes were put down with a superabundance of water and barely a trace of pigment. On solid, cold-pressed paper, 300 grams per square metre, Peter could afford to lay on water like a fireman. He used sable and 'finest sable' brushes, occasionally ox and sable, or hog. He bought most of his paint in Cornelissen & Son, the old artists' colourmen in Great Russell Street, a short walk from the LRB. He had an impressive range of drawing inks – vermilion, yellow, orange and bright green.

Among a large body of work that was never intended for the

LRB, built up over the years with no end in view but painting, there is a self-portrait, which hangs in the Campbells' kitchen. The likeness is unmistakable, yet the sitter is uncharacteristically stern. Peter would often fix his gaze on you as he seems to here, peering over his half-moon spectacles. In life the effect was nearly always quizzical, as though there were still something about an English person, or even a generic Brit, that appeared to him despite his years as a Londoner both engagingly novel and vaguely specious. That disarming expression had none of the severity we find in the eyes and the forehead of the self-portrait, or even the mouth.

Of a self-portrait by the American artist Alice Neel from the 1970s, Peter said that 'the face is rather tight around the mouth, as a painter's face can be when reaching a decision about just how a detail seen in the mirror can be put down with the next stroke.' There's a similar tension in Peter's face under his own scrutiny: this is not the gregarious, inquisitive Peter with his eyes and wits so very much about him. It is the focused twin, the decision-maker, full of 'contained, serious concentration' – Peter again, on a self-portrait by the Scottish painter David Wilkie.

The left hand, which gestured affably in company and now looks like a right hand – this is also a painting of a reflection – is hidden from view, an irrelevant detail. The right hand has been active on the shaded half of the head and face (the viewer's right), where there is plentiful use of wet on wet, the colour dropped onto the moistened paper; the lit half (the viewer's left) is patiently glazed, one layer on an earlier layer that's been left to dry, and so on, with a precision that explains why the person in the picture is more intense and less convivial than the one who could walk into a room and engage almost anybody in conversation. Plenty of artists tackle the self-portrait sooner or later as a technical challenge or a conceit with a couple of passport photos. Peter played it straight.

Peter's father, Arnold, was an educationalist, close to the New Zealand Labour Party, who went on to become head of the New Zealand Council for Educational Research in 1939 and eventually, in 1960, director of the Department of Education. Peter's mother, Nancy Combs, was a founding member of the New Zealand Family Planning Association. Both parents had come through the 1930s convinced of the need to extend education in all areas of life to all areas of society. Peter made less of university than his father had. After a desultory two years studying philosophy, geology and a handful of peripheral subjects, he began serving an apprenticeship with the printer and poet Denis Glover. On completing his final year as a part-time student he picked up work with the New Zealand Schools Publications department, where both parents had connections. He and his wife, Win Doogue, left for Britain in 1960. His earnings in New Zealand from books for young readers paid the rent in London and eventually helped the couple buy their house in Southfields.

Geology had suited Peter better than philosophy, but either way he hadn't much liked being taught. From an early age, he'd been an independent rummager. In the front room at Southfields he kept an edition of Rembrandt's paintings and drawings inscribed in his own neat hand 'Peter Campbell 1949'. He'd asked for the book for his twelfth birthday. The plates and prints are all monochrome. Looking at a drawing catalogued as *Negro Band* from 1637, Peter had to colour in, imagining the 'red and yellow chalk' advertised by the caption. Or the 'watercolour' announced under a picture of *Two Negro Drummers Mounted on Mules*.

Years later, asked why he'd moved to Britain, he said it was a voyage of discovery: he wanted to experience the colours of paintings he'd only seen in black and white. The limitations of books were as clear to him as their advantages. Peter was a keen reader with wide interests. His mother, Nancy, had a passion for Henry James, which he acquired and passed on to his daughter, Jane, who returned the favour by keeping him up to date with contemporary fiction. His son, Ben, put a steady stream of younger writers his way. Ever since his time with Glover at the Wingfield Press in Wellington, books had shaped the contours of Peter's working life and his leisure. He was alert to the way they settled in the hand and met the requirements of a reader's eye.

In the late 1960s he was still turning out children's books, with Jane and Ben in mind. Methuen published three titles written and illustrated by their father. By now he was also designing books for the BBC, always quick to spot an asset, and by 1969 he had become the corporation's main man for 'the book of the film', or rather the series. He was assigned to

M.F. Burnyeat: The Truth about Pythagoras

London Review
OF BOOKS

VOLUME 29 NUMBER 4 · 22 FEBRUARY 2007 · £2.95 US & CANADA $4.95

'It is hard to let go of
Pythagoras. He has
meant so much to so
many for so long. I can
with confidence say to
readers of this essay:
most of what you believe,
or think you know, about Pythagoras is
fiction, much of it deliberately contrived. Did
he discover the geometrical theorem that bears
his name? No. Did he ponder the harmony of the
spheres? Certainly not . . . Does he even deserve
credit for his most famous accomplishment,
analysing the mathematical ratios that structure
musical concordances? Possibly, but . . .'

the blockbusters of public broadcasting in its golden age and told to reconfigure them in print with the help of the presenters: Kenneth Clark on *Civilisation* (1969), Jacob Bronowksi on *The Ascent of Man* (1973) and later, David Attenborough's *Life on Earth* (1979).

Between assignments, Peter found time to design a superb edition of Reynolds Stone's engravings from John Murray. The grabby, mannered styles of the 1970s did mainstream publishing few favours and the BBC jackets, unlike the Reynolds Stone, have not aged gracefully. All the same, Peter knew how to organise blocks of information, lay out a page and set up an illustration as master or servant of the exposition in hand. His writers were indebted to him. Clark inscribed his copy of *Civilisation* 'to Peter Campbell, the perfect editor, from a grateful author'.

It helped that Peter was a fonts-and-faces enthusiast of a high order. He was willing to concede, Diana Souhami wrote in an obituary for the *Guardian*, 'that a book set in the 1790s should have an eighteenth-century typeface'; at the same time he could spot the best of the new type designers emerging in the age of desktop publishing. No proper book design without a knowledge of typography, and Peter's went back a good way. In his teens in Wellington he would have seen the new Penguin covers introduced by Tschichold during his brief heyday at the firm as titles were added to the family library. By the time he reached London, the German engraver Berthold Wolpe was the figure in the ascendant. Wolpe had devised a serif typeface known as Albertus, which Peter greatly admired. During the war, having been deported to Australia and then returned, Wolpe was taken on at Faber & Faber and remained there for thirty years or more, with 1,500 jacket covers to his credit.

Peter took a keen interest in the development of book design. Asked to contribute to a volume of the *Cambridge History of the Book in Britain*, he wrote about the first edition of *Leviathan*, pointing up the use of different fonts to signal themes and sub-themes, and guide the reader through the text from its list of contents to its conclusion. It was, he wrote, like being led through a magnificent house: 'The effect is architectural. The reader is never lost, never unaware of how each wing and the rooms it contains relate to the whole building.'

In Karl Miller's day, the masthead of the LRB was set in a version of Caslon and the columns in Times. In 1997 Peter had a chance to review these arrangements. He shrunk the size of the paper slightly, let the masthead stand and set the pages in Quadraat, a crisp typeface devised by the Dutch designer Fred Smeijers. Quadraat, as Robin Kinross remarked, was 'a tool in a larger strategy': Peter had transformed the look of the LRB and in doing so made it a showcase for Smeijers's elegant design. 'I have said this many times in lectures,' Smeijers wrote to Kinross in 2011, 'the most faithful user of Quadraat is the LRB, or Peter ... Then I show the public some slides of the LRB, [including] a slide of a page with four columns of just Quadraat, no illustrations whatsoever, stating ... that this is one of the most beautiful pages of [pure] text you can get these days, and it comes every two weeks!' Unlike the editors or the publisher, Smeijers was exhilarated if he came across an issue where advertisements were thin on the ground: 'By the way,' he wrote to Kinross, 'in the last LRB there is a spread of two pages, with no illustrations, so eight columns of just Quadraat. If possible do not throw this issue away.'

In the 1990s, Peter was involved in design and typography for the *Musical Times* and *Early Music*, a journal published by Oxford, and for Profile Books. The Fourth Estate logo, also his, was by now a familiar sight in bookshops. He had been collaborating on Quentin Blake's books since the 1980s and later wrote the introduction to *The Life of Birds* (2005). Every autumn his posters went up in museums, galleries and universities, advertising the Pannizi Lectures at the British Library.

In 2000 an issue of *New Left Review* appeared with an introductory essay by Perry Anderson calling for 'uncompromising realism' among the remains of the left. The journal looked and felt quite different. Anderson, who took over the helm for the next few years, had nominated Peter for the redesign. The brief had gone out, the current editor Susan Watkins explained in a piece after Peter's death, at 'a conjuncture transformed by the West's Cold War victory', though had it been put to Peter in quite those terms, he might have been excused for thinking they'd picked the wrong man. In fact, the result was another kind of victory. The calming effect of the Campbell aesthetic lightened what had become a daunting journal. Peter opened up the margins and set about a massive decongestion. Scala, the clean, disinterested typeface he chose, was the invention of another Dutch typographer, Martin Majoor: Peter used it to

PAUL KLEE THE NATURE OF CREATION

bring measure and equanimity to the page. At Anderson's suggestion, he reproduced the letters 'n', 'l', 'r' in brush and watercolour – lower case – and digitised the result for the covers. Before long he was invited to design books for the journal's imprint, Verso.

Peter's most rewarding designs, in his own eyes, were probably his exhibition catalogues. Besides the Klee in 2002, there were two memorable catalogues for the Hayward: *Francis Bacon: The Human Body*, a show curated in 1998 by David Sylvester, a longstanding contributor to the LRB with whom he'd already collaborated, and *Goya: Drawings from His Private Albums* in 2001. Work at the National Gallery now came his way via the publishing director Kate Bell, who'd moved on from the Hayward. Together they produced a short book on Vermeer to coincide with a major show. A run of commissions followed, with exhibitions of Kitaj, Titian, El Greco, Rubens and Cézanne.

The Rubens catalogue was one of Peter's favourites and saw him take charge of the curator's text as well as the design. The challenge of *Rubens: A Master in the Making* was to show how far the young Rubens had relied on classical and Renaissance sculpture (and cannibalised his own pictures) as he beat a path to maturity: with references well beyond the work that was on display, the catalogue had to do more than the usual share of work. Peter's answer was to design it as a viewer's toolkit, or as Bell put it, 'a visual extension of the exhibition'.

Working on the earlier Titian catalogue had allowed him to return at his leisure to the transfiguring brushwork of the master – 'a new way of recording likeness', he wrote in the LRB, 'that would define the technical ambitions of European portrait painting until photography put an end to them'. The text of the Titian catalogue was set in a serif typeface and when promotional pressures required a chunky sans serif for the cover, the jarring contrast became a source of anxiety. It was Peter, Bell remembers, who came up with 'the radical idea of having no title on the cover at all'. The book went on to become one of the gallery's bestselling publications.

NOT ALL PETER'S PLANS went smoothly or came to fruition. One that ran into trouble was *Master Pieces*, a witty, how-to book dreamed up in the early 1980s in collaboration with a British writer, Richard Ball. The idea, in Ball's words, was 'to give readers and makers a new way of approaching paintings' by explaining how to build a piece of furniture depicted in a famous work. The book consists of twenty 'master pieces', lists of materials, instructions for assembly and reproductions of the pictures in which they're to be found: Van Gogh's chair in *Chair and Pipe*, a sideboard from a Picasso still life, a trestle table from *Christ in the House of Simon* by the fifteenth-century Dutch artist Dirk Bouts, the deacon's bed in *The Dream of the Deacon Justinian* by Fra Angelico and so on. Prototypes of all the pieces were built under Peter's supervision and exhibitions were lined up at Hille's showroom in London and the Museum of Modern Art in Oxford.

After Hearst published *Master Pieces* in 1983 a firm of English solicitors representing SPADEM, the royalties and copyright agency in Paris, leapt into action, demanding that the book be withdrawn and all the furniture inspired by twentieth-century pieces destroyed. The exhibitions in the UK went ahead without the modernist items (there was a third show in New York at the Workbench gallery). So did the first print run of the book. However, it was agreed that there should be no further runs, even in the US, where the Picasso was the only contested item. Most of the pre-twentieth-century prototypes survive. Someone somewhere owns a facsimile of Mme Récamier's chaise longue, which set her off to such startling effect – the gloved hand, as it were, without the proffered string of pearls – and someone owns the Virgin's elaborate lectern from Ghirlandaio's *Annunciation* in the Baptistery loggia at San Gimignano. The condemned pieces were never destroyed: they found their way discreetly into people's homes, where they remain – including a handsome version of the table from *The Difficult Crossing* (the 1926 version) by Magritte. SPADEM fell into disrepute and folded in the mid-1990s.

Peter's private works for friends and family carried fewer liabilities: over many years he turned out decorated notebooks, address books and hand-painted postcards. He also wrote a very brief guide to composition, in the form of an illustrated letter to Anna Fender, the daughter of friends, consisting of notes on a selection of photos he'd taken in Italy. Though he excelled at 'looking and noticing', he suggested to Anna that they were not 'the only reasons for making pictures'. She should also understand that 'all makers of images borrow from each other.' He

Saxifraga Aizoon rosea / x

Paeonia Mlokosewitchi

Spiraea elegantissima x

Uniola latifolia

grass *Mixed om. grasses*

Cordaleria argentia

Primula auricula Alpine yell

Orchis Morio

Dryas octopetala

juxtaposed a shot of a basket of fruit on a tiled floor and another of flowering mustard beside some olive trees:

> These are now two of the commonest kinds of picture – landscape and still life. There was a time when people would have expected them to be about something (particularly the landscape) . . . The pictures are very simple, much simpler than the world. I took the fruit basket off the table so the picture would be just of it and the wall and the tiles, and I avoided getting any houses or the road or people into the landscape.

From the reading of genres to the workaday detail, Peter's thoughts move freely but the passage ends with an emphatic tribute to two of his favourite painters: 'Lots of paintings work by making less stand for more. But getting hold of the complexity of the world, getting in everything as Bonnard, say, or Rubens sometimes seems to, is the best and most difficult game.'

Peter used his own notebooks to work up sketches for covers and jot down thoughts about the shows he noticed for the LRB. There's also more personal material. In a book from the end of the 1960s he kept lists of seeds and shrubs to be ordered from nurseries along with their prices ('Mahonia japonica, 1/6d' etc), interspersed with pen-and-ink sketches, including a plan of the back garden in Southfields, with newly ordered plants imagined in their places.

The loveliest of his books is a red Moleskine volume, which he began to fill about forty years later. By now he'd become impatient with manicured natural forms and the tampering human hand. Gardens were no longer so interesting. 'In my seventy-first year,' he writes in 2008, 'I find I want to know about plants,' and goes on to say that he'd like to live among them 'as anthropologists live among the natives of isolated tribes, to learn but not to interfere'. Walking near the Cheshire-Flintshire border, he sees nothing 'that has the self-sorted natural balance of unmanaged landscape'. He tells himself: '*Read Rackham on managed/wild woodland.*'

Oliver Rackham's books on woodland ecologies were among several delights he'd already savoured and now meant to return to. Others included a long treatise on the graminae (Peter loved to paint grass and walk in it up to his shins), a study by E. J. H. Corner of *The Life of Plants* and *The British Islands and Their Vegetation* by A. G. Tansley, all three of which he owned. In the meantime he'd obtained a translation of Ray's *Catalogus Plantarum circa*

Cantabrigiam Nascentium (1600), and transcribed a line from the preface, addressed to 'men of University standing': from time to time, it advised, they should renounce the library and wander outdoors to 'gain wisdom by their own experience rather than from somebody else's brain'. Peter added: 'If you are to write about vegetation, that must be your guide.' His wish to know was inseparable from the wish to set it down.

Peter's intention, to judge from the notes, was a book based on his findings as an inexhaustible walker, observer and recorder, out on the common, about in the wilder fringes of the back garden, wandering away from the towpath at Putney, or moving gingerly on the limestone pavement of the White Peak, examining mosses. The book would consist of careful, luminous description. The business of setting out to see and describe would also be brought into focus, as a short passage in his notes implies: 'Coleridge and Will. & Dot. Wordsworth in the Quantocks, sitting on camp stools with portfolios, noting down the look of things.'

But poets were not the guiding lights for this piece of work and neither were artists. Peter had become interested instead in the figure of the amateur naturalist, who could account for the 'look of things' in the process of capturing it. 'Amateur'? Peter, a competent professional – designer, critic and draughtsman – now meant to write about plant life as if from an open-access tradition. 'Any science I describe,' he notes, 'must be at a distant second-hand but observation of specifics is, to a degree, my practice.' But who or what was a professional in this eclectic area of study? The answer: 'Natural history – the amateur pursuit – is a constant avocation like reading.'

By now, he had begun to think of the world as a vast lending library where members who took out plenty of titles and worked through them would find satisfaction and instruction, and pass these on in their own distinctive ways. Borrowing had become the mark of intelligence and engagement. In his jottings on a show at the British Museum, he writes of artists working with 'the borrowed science of perspective' and by the time he's reached the realm of natural history, he seems to see a baggy discipline, with a sharp eye and sensible shoes, destined even so to spend much of its time indoors, roaming the stacks and scavenging from other disciplines – evolutionary science, geology, the arts – in order to ground the enchantments of fieldwork.

57 MAY/JUNE 2009

NEW LEFT REVIEW

Perry Anderson   *Land of Ideas?*
Slavoj Žižek   *Class and Commons*
Roberto Schwarz   *Staging the Crash*
Alain Supiot   *Possible Europes*
Immanuel Wallerstein   *Reflections on Fanon*
Alexander Zevin   *Reordering 68*
Chin-tao Wu   *Biennials Sans Frontières*
Tom Hazeldine   *England's Revolution*
R. Taggart Murphy   *Beyond Bubblenomics*

Leo Panitch & Martijn Konings
Myths of Neoliberal Deregulation

'To have been asked to write, draw and design for the paper over the years,' Peter wrote in his preface to *At...*, 'has been my great, my absurd, good fortune.' But it was more than good fortune. Among contributors, the trials of writing for the LRB were legendary in Karl's Miller's day and got no easier as time went on. Anxieties were heightened for staffers – Peter was one – who hadn't been hired to write in the first place but sooner or later found themselves with assignments: what were they doing in print, in the company of writers whose reputations sold the paper? Peter was unruffled. He could knock out strong, democratic pieces that took you through a gallery or walked you round a building with a quiet authority and the merest hint that you might have something to learn. In due course his writing became a valuable deposit in the fine arts layer of *LRB* geology, alongside work by critics like William Feaver and Tom Lubbock, and essays by scholars and artists whose names he'd presented many times on the cover: David Sylvester, Nicholas Penny, T. J. Clark, Julian Bell, Bridget Riley, Hal Foster, Rosalind Krauss, Richard Wollheim. By and large he chose his own subjects and set his own pace. Going over his copy, you heard no fast food rumblings: he never had to bolt down a piece of information at the last minute. He had lived with the material he described for most of his life. Every two weeks he disappeared with an assignment and then he reappeared; he met his deadlines; he was a model journalist.

In her farewell to Peter in NLR, Susan Watkins spotted one of his great articles, from 2010, about a show of Renaissance drawings at the British Museum. In his opening paragraph, Peter went at once to the process of production: the exorbitant cost of materials, the need for constant experiment, how artists squirrelled away successful sketches, like money in the bank, to be recycled in later projects, until the arrival of printing, whereupon old bits of paper and vellum where studies jostled for valuable space ceased to be such a crucial workshop resource. He asked his readers to imagine the economy of drawing and painting in a Renaissance atelier. And then to consider how many options had to be tested before a work could get fully under way. In preliminary sketches for the San Benedetto altarpiece by Lorenzo Monaco in the National Gallery, he noticed, the figures had been 'moved about like chessmen'.

Here he is on another kind of economy – the economy of lifestyles – and the old bachelor habits which artists on both sides of the Channel were able to cultivate with the help of wealthy patrons:

> Delacroix should be an open book to the British. He respected them. He was a dandy with a taste for English clothes. The English taught him to paint in watercolour ... While others crossed the Alps to see Rome, Delacroix crossed the Channel to England and rather liked it ... There are no longer, I would guess, enough energetic hostesses – amusing people with time on their hands, cooks, parlour maids and untaxed income – for any substantial part of society to indulge in the abundant entertaining which underpinned bachelor life of the old kind ... Henry James, Proust and Degas were all, like Delacroix, supported by it. When they went home it was to a housekeeper and the muse – who, Delacroix wrote, 'is a jealous mistress. She abandons you at the slightest infidelity.'

Peter liked to explain how ambitious works of art came about, as he does in a piece on Bonnard's paintings, locating their origins partly in the dream of colour, partly in the rapid sketches he made in his pocket diaries:

> These drawings from life were the seeds from which the paintings grew. But they were painted from the imagination. 'I have all my subjects to hand,' [Bonnard] is recorded as saying: 'I go and look at them. I take notes. Then I go home. Before I start painting, I reflect, I dream.' Colour ... was deployed to produce an image that gives a sense of the taste of ordinary life, but almost every line has been adjusted, experimented with, recharged ... Bonnard himself said he could not paint from nature because he ... had no defence before the facts of the thing in front of him. It had first to be reflected on, 'dreamed'.

The 'distinctiveness' of artists was an idea he approached with caution, but when he'd seen it, as he did in Joan Eardley, he had no difficulty accounting for it:

> In her land and seascapes Eardley knifes, drips and brushes paint with broad gestures which ... resemble those of Tachiste contemporaries. Hans Hartung and Pierre Soulages were both painters whose work she could have seen exhibited in Scotland. More to the point are the abstracted landscapes of Nicolas de Staël and Soutine's crumpled, wavy transformations of Céret ... 'Provincial' is a condescending word ... but I can't think of a better one to describe a particular kind of distance from the traffic of styles and reputations that Eardley exemplifies. It is not that she was unknown outside

Thomas Laqueur: The Illustrious Dead

London Review
OF BOOKS

VOLUME 23 NUMBER 18 20 SEPTEMBER 2001 £2.95 US & CANADA $3.95

Colm Tóibín: The Talents of James Baldwin
Julian Bell: Sickert lays about him
August Kleinzahler: Too Bad about Mrs Ferri
R.W. Johnson: Hey, hey, Henry K.

Elizabeth Lowry: Alistair MacLeod's Family Legends
Thomas Nagel: Are lemons really yellow?
Tom Shippey: Icelanders go viking
Alison Jolly: Proud to be a Primate

Scotland or ignorant of what was going on in the world. She made regular trips to London to see exhibitions ... But the self-confidence that carried her forward, undistracted by the strong international currents that broke the flow of other careers, seems to have been sustained by attachment to her native place.

In another piece he retraces the route that led Samuel Palmer into a 'hermetic world, essentially an illustrator's world', whose scale and ambitions made him a more approachable artist, to Peter's mind, than William Blake:

> In the compelling self-portrait drawing of around 1824–25, as memorable as any by an English artist, he seems both vulnerable and determined. He was then just out of his teens; a couple of years earlier he had been sought out by an older artist, John Linnell, who had seen and admired his work. Palmer wrote that God had sent Linnell 'to pluck me from the pit of modernity'. Through Linnell ... Palmer met William Blake. It was the light of Blake and the old prints Linnell pointed him towards – in particular those of Dürer, Lucas van Leyden and Bonasone – that showed Palmer the path out of the pit of modernity.

And then there are the walks, which he staged as guided tours for himself and his readers. Here he returns to New Zealand to consider the way a built environment looks when its inhabitants think nothing of moving around, and sometimes take their houses with them:

> I am in Wellington, where I spent my first twenty years. I have walked, as I used to then, down the hill from Wadestown ... Houses speckle the steep green hills around the harbour more thickly than they did in the past, because pieces of land so close to vertical that you would not trust yourself to scramble down them are now built on, as are plots perched on the fault scarp itself. Houses are tucked in or cantilevered out, the carports and backs ... are supported on stilts, and verandahs and decks project over long drops, down to roofs or bush below. Zigzag paths and steep steps cut up and down the hillsides ... Timber-frame houses are light: you can move them about – people quite often do. In a lot to the north of the city you can see dozens of bungalows – even a few two-storey houses – lined up like second-hand cars ... If you grow up among houses which are lightly tied to the ground moving them seems almost as natural as shuffling furniture around inside.

But under Peter's inquisitive eye it was the destiny of all built environments to appear mobile, or at least conspire with movement, and he disliked the proliferation of electric lighting in London because it brought the city to an ugly standstill. At Christmas, he wrote, 'the kinds of thing that are done with light are very like those which, if done with a spray-can, would have boys up in front of the magistrates.' Buildings should be seen 'by the shifting light of day (sometimes bright, sometimes flattened by cloud, low in the morning and evening, high at noon, varying from season to season and hour to hour, but always coming from above or from the side)'. Switched on in the early evening and turned off after dawn, lighting made it harder to explore the physiognomy of a façade. Floodlit from below, it became a grimace. 'Think how you would feel,' he wrote, 'about the performances of an actor who had to do half of them with a torch held under his chin.'

Fortunately there were all kinds of modulations to be observed in the thoroughfares and pavements of the city, as he explained in this piece about streets:

> Roadmaking, not the most glamorous civil engineering project, deserves respect. To the engineer a puddle is a reprimand. It is his or her job to see that water is guided towards drains. That requires slopes at very small angles: the shallow curve of the tarmac carriageway, the gentle slope of the pavement, the modest incline of the gutter towards the drain. When you see pavement slabs being laid it looks as though they are being tapped down onto a foundation of sand. In fact it is weak cement: delicate enough to be broken up easily when a new pipe is laid, coherent enough to keep out the water that could wash it away and leave the slab rocking.

And then, looking up for a moment: 'Pedestrians, like birds in circling flocks, are remarkably good at avoiding one another.' Navigating around Peter during his inspections of the ground beneath his feet would have called for special skills on the part of fellow pedestrians.

The pleasure he took in these urban field trips resonates in his findings. As it does in less risky assignments, like his study of the 1651 *Leviathan* – so carefully organised, he decided, that the edition was both 'an illustration and a diagram of its contents'. This close coincidence of form and function, with its hint of tautology – the thing being the guide to itself – was part of what intrigued him about natural history, amateur or not. For all its impressive bustle – looking, reading, drafting, naming – he was more convinced by the 'self-sorted balance' of the plant species, which seemed to him to illustrate themselves and divulge their own order. And yet, to Peter's great delight, the naturalists had never given up their 'gathering and describing', as he wrote in a piece about the early stirrings of natural history: 'sustained by habits of curiosity and close observation' they scribbled away in the margins of the book of nature. Peter, too, was never without a pencil or paper and shared that consuming interest in the natural world, for all his love of man-made things. He could bring close observation to bear on a wooded valley in the Auvergne, a Dutch masterpiece or a manhole cover. As for curiosity, he had no end of it.

Some of the pictures towards the end of this book are from Peter's own portfolio. They include several landscapes, a vase of anemones in pastels, a still life in oils, and an occasional piece with a dog in a pram, dedicated to his wife, Win, for their wedding anniversary or her birthday – Peter had confused the two.

At... writing from the 'London Review of Books' was published by Hyphen in 2009. The first illustrated edition of C.J. Holmes, *Notes on the Science of Picture-Making*, was published by Chatto & Windus in 1927. The title of the essay in the *Cambridge History of the Book in Britain, Vol IV, 1557–1695* (Bernard & McKenzie 2002) is 'The Typography of Hobbes's *Leviathan*'. Susan Watkins's article appeared in the November/December 2011 issue of *New Left Review*. Some of Peter Campbell's pieces in the LRB, excerpted here, are freely available on the paper's website; all can be revisited by subscribers.

LRB Covers

GALEN STRAWSON: Immortality!

London Review
OF BOOKS

VOLUME 33 NUMBER 11   2 JUNE 2011   £3.20 US & CANADA $4.95

JACKSON LEARS: God loves America

London Review
OF BOOKS

VOLUME 33 NUMBER 10   19 MAY 2011   £3.20 US & CANADA $4.95

JOHN LANCHESTER: Any hope for the euro?

London Review
OF BOOKS

VOLUME 33 NUMBER 14   14 JULY 2011   £3.20 US & CANADA $4.95

ADAM SHATZ: The No-State Solution
ANTHONY GRAFTON: Himmler's Tacitus
ANDREW O'HAGAN: Beryl Bainbridge

JOHN LANCHESTER: THE BANKS

London Review
OF BOOKS

VOLUME 31 NUMBER 10   28 MAY 2009   £3.20 US & CANADA $4.95

David Runciman:
The Future of
Wikipedia

Anne Enright:
A Writer's
Life

Charles Nicholl:
Colonel Fawcett's
Signet Ring

Hal Foster: Libeskind in New York

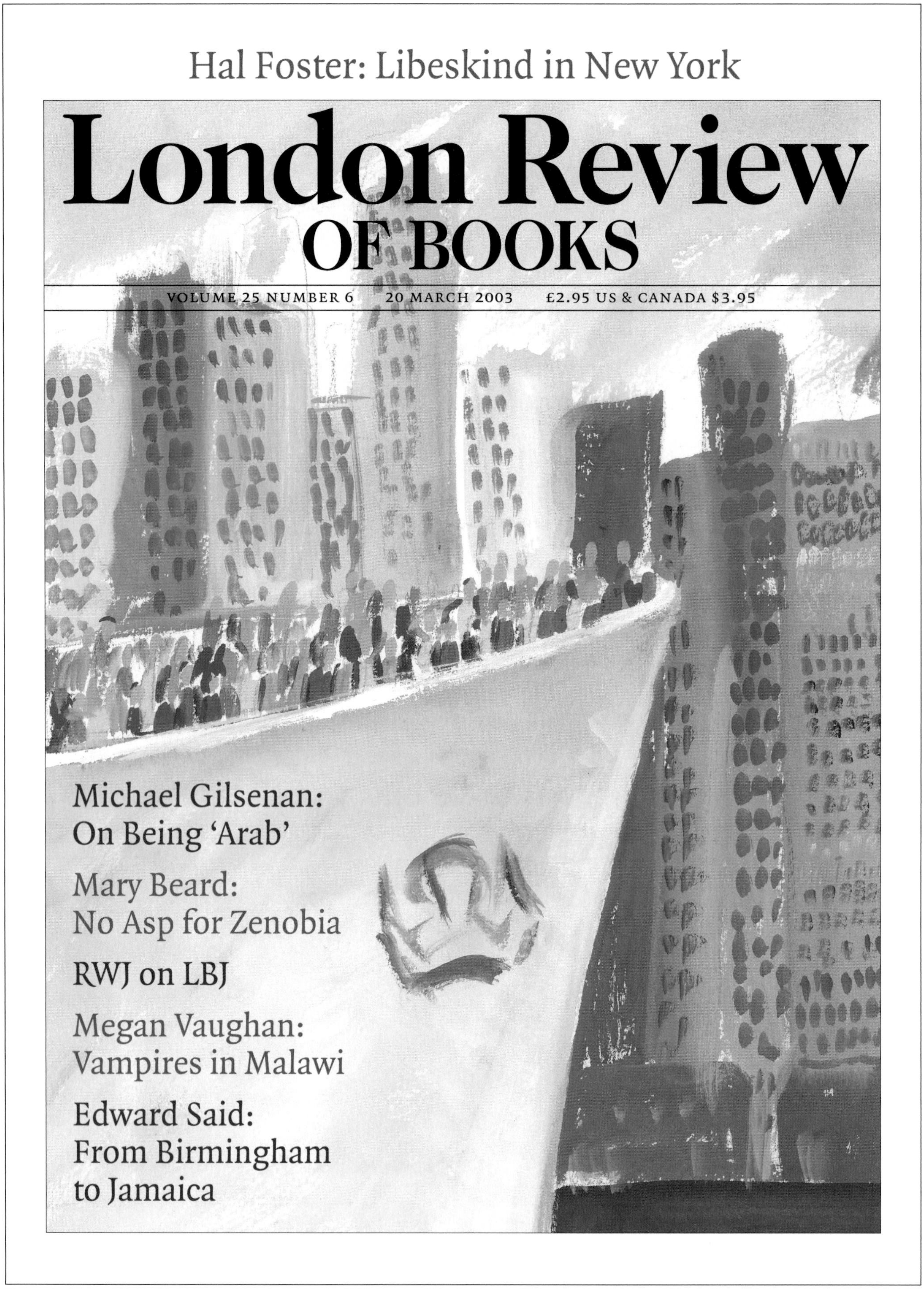

London Review OF BOOKS

VOLUME 25 NUMBER 6 20 MARCH 2003 £2.95 US & CANADA $3.95

Michael Gilsenan: On Being ‘Arab’

Mary Beard: No Asp for Zenobia

RWJ on LBJ

Megan Vaughan: Vampires in Malawi

Edward Said: From Birmingham to Jamaica

Frank Lentricchia: Four Fictions

London Review
OF BOOKS

VOLUME 20 NUMBER 22   12 NOVEMBER 1998   £2.50 US & CANADA $2.95

London Review
OF BOOKS

VOLUME 30 NUMBER 21   6 NOVEMBER 2008   £3.20 US & CANADA $4.95

Jenny Diski on Alastair Campbell's Dodgy Novel
Stephen Burt: The Poetry of Frank Bidart
Sanjay Subrahmanyam: Another Booker Flop

London Review
OF BOOKS

VOLUME 32 NUMBER 13   8 JULY 2010   £3.20 US & CANADA $4.95

Michael Wood:
Borges

Thomas Laqueur:
Trauma

Jenny Diski:
Arsenic

David Kaiser:
Aliens

Christopher Hitchens: So, farewell then, Richard Nixon

London Review
OF BOOKS

VOLUME 16 NUMBER 14   21 JULY 1994   £2.15 US & CANADA $2.95

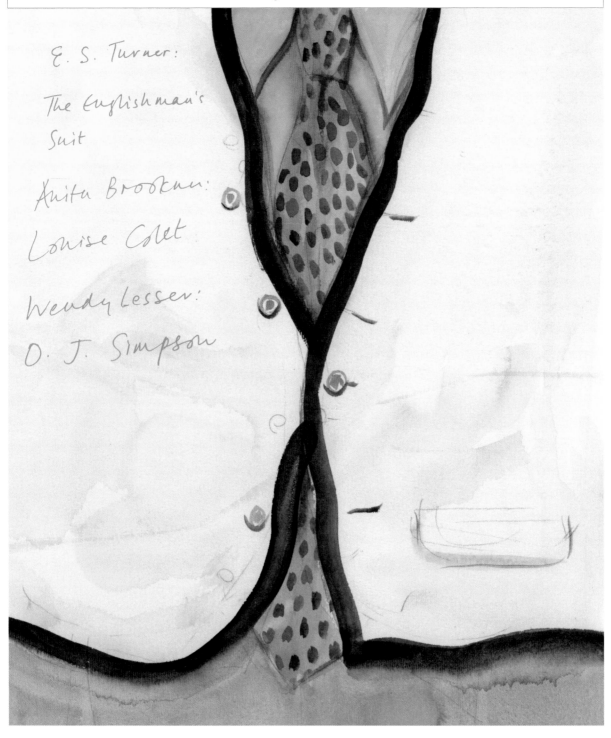

London Review
OF BOOKS

VOLUME 17 NUMBER 15   3 AUGUST 1995   £2.15 US & CANADA $2.95

Fredric Jameson on Walter Benjamin

Edward Luttwak:
In Praise of Theft

R.W. Johnson:
Major Wins the Losership

Four Poems by
Ian Hamilton

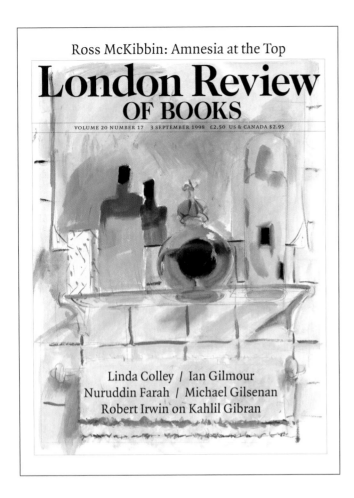

Ross McKibbin: Amnesia at the Top

London Review
OF BOOKS

VOLUME 20 NUMBER 17   3 SEPTEMBER 1998   £2.50 US & CANADA $2.95

Linda Colley / Ian Gilmour
Nuruddin Farah / Michael Gilsenan
Robert Irwin on Kahlil Gibran

Alan Bennett's Diary for 1996

London Review
OF BOOKS

VOLUME 19 NUMBER 1   2 JANUARY 1997   £2.25 US & CANADA $2.95

Jenny Diski: Mrs Freud

London Review
OF BOOKS

VOLUME 28 NUMBER 6   23 MARCH 2006   £2.99 US & CANADA $3.95

'Other special-interest groups
have managed to skew foreign
policy, but no lobby has managed
to divert it as far from what the
national interest would suggest,
while simultaneously convincing
Americans that US interests and
Israel's are essentially identical.'

John Mearsheimer and Stephen Walt
on the Israel Lobby

Frank Kermode on Blasphemy

London Review
OF BOOKS

VOLUME 24 NUMBER 2   24 JANUARY 2002   £2.95 US & CANADA $3.95

'VERY FEW friendships can survive your saying: "I like you but I don't like your poems." Much better to say: "I don't like you but I like your poems." Yes, that would have been OK.'

Ian Hamilton

Alan Bennett: Fresh Revelations

London Review
OF BOOKS

VOLUME 16 NUMBER 20   20 OCTOBER 1994   £2.15 US & CANADA $2.95

John Bayley   Dinah Birch   Marilyn Butler   David Cannadine
Allen Curnow   Jenny Diski   Stephen Greenblatt
Ian Hamilton   Dave Haslam   Christopher Hitchens
Michael Hofmann   R.W. Johnson   Frank Kermode
Ross McKibbin   Hilary Mantel   Richard Rorty   Edward Said
Stephen Sedley   Elaine Showalter   Iain Sinclair
David Sylvester   Bernard Williams   Michael Wood

THIRTIETH ANNIVERSARY ISSUE

London Review
OF BOOKS

VOLUME 31 NUMBER 21   5 NOVEMBER 2009   £3.20 US & CANADA $4.95

Jacqueline Rose:
Honour Killing

1979

Jonathan Raban:
Reading Empson

Colm Tóibín:
John Cheever

Thomas Nagel:
I and Me

Jeremy Harding:
Guantánamo

Andrew O'Hagan:
Guilt: A Memoir

Alan Bennett:
The Habit of Art

Daniel Soar:
Sebastian Faulks

Julian Bell:
Van Gogh's Letters

Frank Kermode:
William Golding

Hilary Mantel:
Hypochondria

Jenny Diski:
Rape-Rape

Julian Barnes:
Maupassant

Thomas Jones:
Bio Insecurity

John Lanchester:
Lehman Brothers

Peter Campbell:
Moctezuma

Michael Wood:
Agnès Varda

2009

John Ashbery
Charles Simic

Neal Ascherson: Why the Cold War didn't wipe us out

London Review
OF BOOKS

VOLUME 19 NUMBER 20   16 OCTOBER 1997   £2.50   US & CANADA $2.95

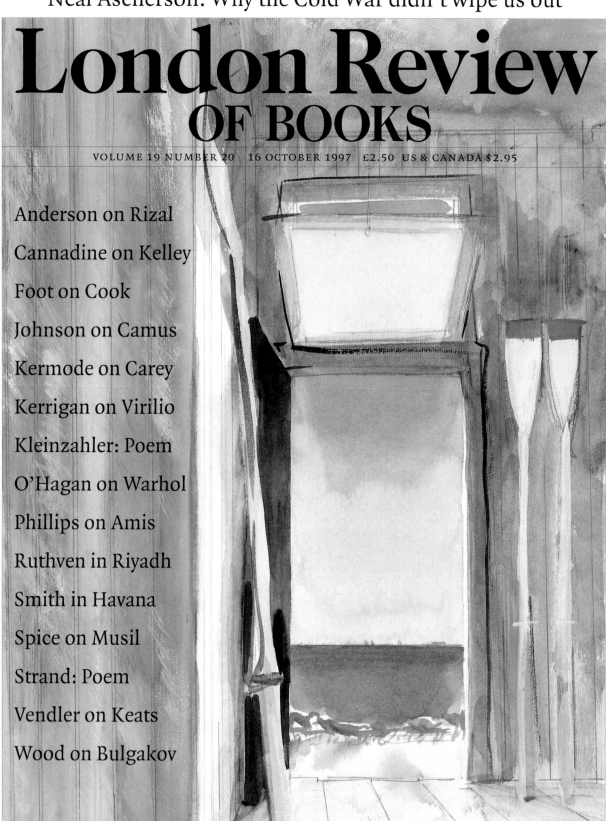

James Davidson: How Good Was Nureyev?

London Review
OF BOOKS

VOLUME 29 NUMBER 23   29 NOVEMBER 2007   £3.20 US & CANADA $4.95

Greg Grandin: Henry Kissinger's Vanity
Tom Paulin: Ted Hughes and the Hare
Mark Ford: Elizabeth Bishop's Toucan
T.C. Smout: What Makes an Oak Tree Grow

Benedict Anderson in Laos

London Review
OF BOOKS

VOLUME 20 NUMBER 12   18 JUNE 1998   £2.50 US & CANADA $2.95

David Bromwich

Ian Hamilton

Lorna Sage

John Sturrock

Mary Beard

Adam Phillips

Penelope Fitzgerald

Eqbal Ahmad

Edwin Morgan

James Davidson

Marina Warner

A.L. Kennedy

John Mullan

Tom Paulin

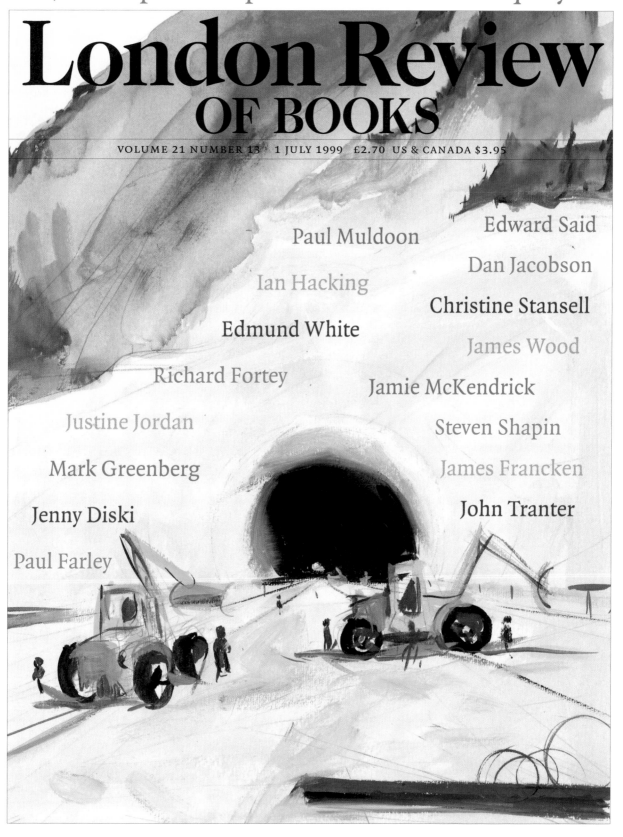

John Upton reopens the Lawrence Inquiry

London Review
OF BOOKS

VOLUME 21 NUMBER 13   1 JULY 1999   £2.70   US & CANADA $3.95

Paul Muldoon

Ian Hacking

Edmund White

Richard Fortey

Justine Jordan

Mark Greenberg

Jenny Diski

Paul Farley

Edward Said

Dan Jacobson

Christine Stansell

James Wood

Jamie McKendrick

Steven Shapin

James Francken

John Tranter

THE UNINVITED

Refugees at the
Rich Man's Gate

Jeremy Harding

Jeremy Harding: At the Rich Man's Gate

London Review
OF BOOKS

VOLUME 22 NUMBER 3   3 FEBRUARY 2000   £2.75   US & CANADA $3.95

Social security scamming appears to
come low on the list of priorities
for the survivor of an 'anti-terrorist'
operation in Turkish Kurdistan
who leaves his village on horseback,
calls on his cousins, raises the
cost of a passage to sanctuary,
travels by bus and truck to Izmir or
Istanbul, buys a place on a boat to Albania
and, three months later, still in the
hands of a trafficking network, is invited
to step out of a lorry on the A3 and make his
way to a police station in Guildford.

Hilary Mantel: Little Miss Neverwell

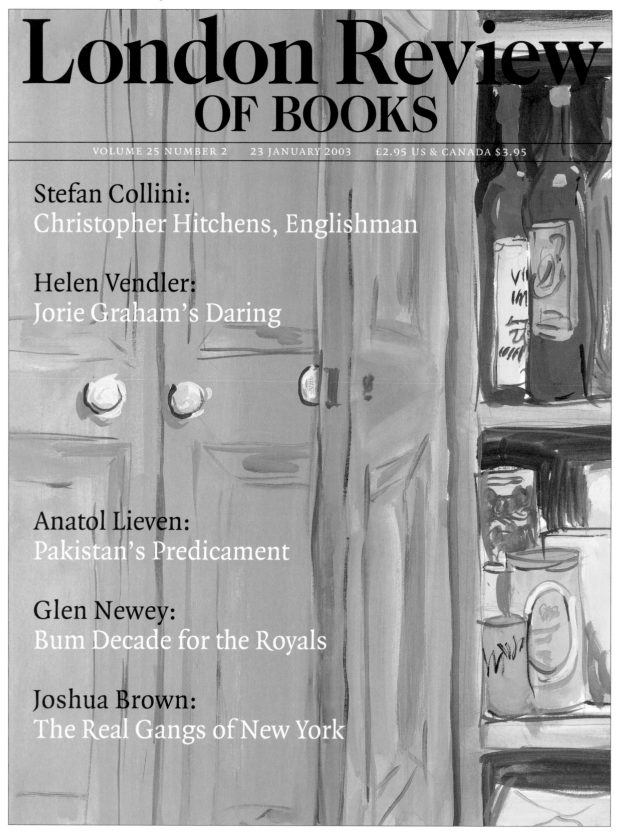

London Review
OF BOOKS

VOLUME 25 NUMBER 2   23 JANUARY 2003   £2.95 US & CANADA $3.95

Tariq Ali: A Secular History of Islam

London Review
OF BOOKS

VOLUME 24 NUMBER 3   7 FEBRUARY 2002   £2.95 US & CANADA $3.95

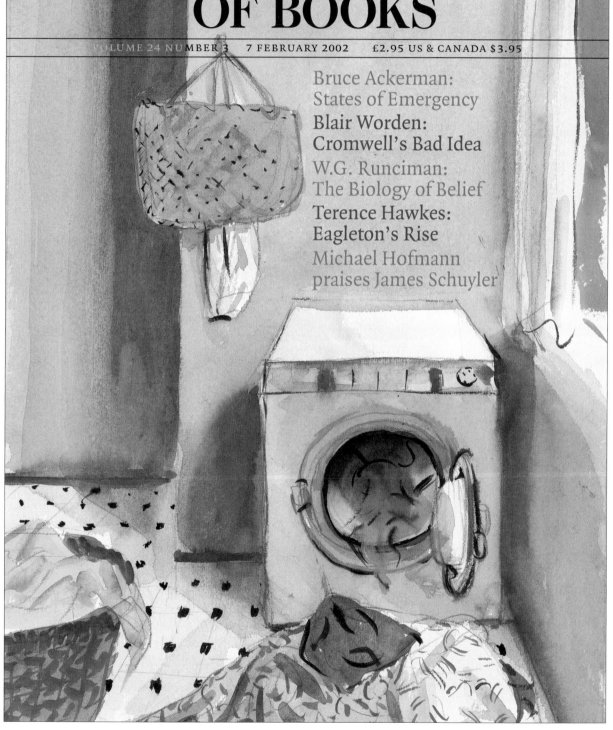

Bruce Ackerman:
States of Emergency

Blair Worden:
Cromwell's Bad Idea

W.G. Runciman:
The Biology of Belief

Terence Hawkes:
Eagleton's Rise

Michael Hofmann
praises James Schuyler

John Lanchester: Marx at 193

London Review
OF BOOKS

VOLUME 34 NUMBER 7   5 APRIL 2012   £3.50 US & CANADA $4.95

ROSS McKIBBIN:
Is that it for the
Lib Dems?

SEAMUS PERRY:
Half-Visionary Art

THOMAS JONES:
Eternal Bowie

ADAM SHATZ:
Claude Lanzmann

EVGENY MOROZOV:
Reading It off Your Face

JEREMY HARDING:
Sarcophagi in
Bordeaux

Murray Sayle goes back to Bloody Sunday

London Review
OF BOOKS

VOLUME 24 NUMBER 13   11 JULY 2002   £2.95 US & CANADA $3.95

John Lanchester: My Sporting Life
Hermione Lee: Coetzee in London
Christopher Hitchens: Crimes against Allende

Ian Hamilton: Snoop Doggy Dogg for Laureate

London Review
OF BOOKS

VOLUME 21 NUMBER 1 7 JANUARY 1999 £2.50 US & CANADA $2.95

Stephen Greenblatt: Disenchantment

Gabriele Annan:
The Lovely Langhornes

Perry Anderson:
Goodbye to Bonn

Penelope Fitzgerald:
Poor John Lehmann

Christopher Hitchens:
The Wrong Stuff

Edward Said: New Palestinians

Paul Foot: Highway Robbery

Wynne Godley: Record of a Nightmare

London Review
OF BOOKS

VOLUME 23 NUMBER 4   22 FEBRUARY 2001   £2.95 US & CANADA $3.95

Frank Kermode: Auden's Shakespeare

Michael Rogin: Josephine Baker

Alan Bennett's Review of the Year

London Review
OF BOOKS

VOLUME 23 NUMBER 2   25 JANUARY 2001   £2.95 US & CANADA $3.95

Stephen Sedley in His Lodgings

London Review
OF BOOKS

VOLUME 21 NUMBER 22   11 NOVEMBER 1999   £2.70   US & CANADA $3.95

SHEILA FITZPATRICK: Was I a spy?

London Review
OF BOOKS

VOLUME 32 NUMBER 23   2 DECEMBER 2010   £3.20 US & CANADA $4.95

T.J. CLARK: Symptoms of Cézannoia
CHARLES NICHOLL: The Bits Shakespeare Wrote

JAMES HARKIN: Tweet for the CIA!
JULIAN BELL: Paint Serious, Paint Big
SANJAY SUBRAHMANYAM: Anarchists in High Places

Seven Essays for a Rainy Summer

London Review
OF BOOKS

VOLUME 20 NUMBER 15   30 JULY 1998   £2.50 US & CANADA $2.95

London Review
OF BOOKS

VOLUME 31 NUMBER 24   17 DECEMBER 2009   £3.20 US & CANADA $4.95

Michael Wood: Frank Kermode • Miranda Carter: Somerset Maugham

Charles Glass scuttles the French fleet • Jérôme Tubiana: Chad at War

R.W. Johnson: The Cup Comes to Cape Town

Matthew Hughes: The Man who Killed Hammarskjöld?

London Review
OF BOOKS

VOLUME 23 NUMBER 15   9 AUGUST 2001   £2.95 US & CANADA $3.95

Nicholas Penny: The Apotheosis of Piero

London Review
OF BOOKS

VOLUME 25 NUMBER 8   17 APRIL 2003   £2.95 US & CANADA $3.95

Hilary Mantel: Children of the Revolution
James Wood on Graham Swift
E.S. Turner: Kiss me, Eric

Edward Said, Charles Glass and others on the war in Iraq
Art Spiegelman: 'In the Shadow of No Towers'

Toril Moi: Beauvoir Misrepresented

London Review
OF BOOKS

VOLUME 32 NUMBER 3   11 FEBRUARY 2010   £3.20 US & CANADA $4.95

Tim Parks: Pavese's Road to Suicide
Stephen Smith: The French Retreat from Africa
James Wood: 'A Hero of Our Time'
Tom McCarthy on Jean-Philippe Toussaint
August Kleinzahler Sells His Childhood Home

Ian Hacking: The Age of Transplants

London Review
OF BOOKS

VOLUME 28 NUMBER 24   14 DECEMBER 2006   £2.99 US & CANADA $4.95

Peter Mair: What's going on in Holland?

Lorna Scott Fox: Chile's Women   John Bossy: Marlowe Cleared!

John Lanchester: The Black Art   Stefan Collini: Kingsley Amis

London Review
OF BOOKS

VOLUME 27 NUMBER 2   20 JANUARY 2005   £2.99 US & CANADA $3.95

Richard Rorty:
After Kripke

Colin Burrow:
Whatever
happened to
Stephen
Greenblatt?

Ian Gilmour:
Wordsworth
Unread

Art Spiegelman:
Mood Indigo

James Davidson: Why would a guy want to marry a guy?

London Review
OF BOOKS

VOLUME 27 NUMBER 11   2 JUNE 2005   £2.99 US & CANADA $3.95

Gareth Peirce: The War on British Muslims

London Review
OF BOOKS

VOLUME 30 NUMBER 7   10 APRIL 2008   £3.20 US & CANADA $4.95

Elif Batuman: Superheroes   David Bromwich: President-Speak
Jeremy Waldron: The One Per Cent Doctrine   Lewis Siegelbaum:
Communist Morality Wendy Doniger: Ekwos, Equus, Aśva, Eoh

Jenny Turner: The Hobbit Habit

London Review
OF BOOKS

VOLUME 23 NUMBER 22   15 NOVEMBER 2001   £2.95 US & CANADA $3.95

Alfred Appel Jr: Homage to Fats Waller

London Review
OF BOOKS

VOLUME 24 NUMBER 9   9 MAY 2002   £2.95 US & CANADA $3.95

Terry Castle on the 20th Century's Most Fabulous Woman

London Review
OF BOOKS

VOLUME 20 NUMBER 5   5 MARCH 1998   £2.50 US & CANADA $2.95

Michael Hofmann: Read Robert Lowell!

London Review
OF BOOKS

VOLUME 25 NUMBER 17   11 SEPTEMBER 2003   £2.99 US & CANADA $3.95

Stefan Collini: How innocent was Stephen Spender?

London Review
OF BOOKS

VOLUME 26 NUMBER 14   22 JULY 2004   £2.99 US & CANADA $3.95

Jeremy Harding: The Banlieues Go to the Polls

London Review
OF BOOKS

VOLUME 29 NUMBER 8   26 APRIL 2007   £2.99 US & CANADA $4.95

Christopher Tayler: Among the New Tories
Eric Hobsbawm: Communism in Britain
Colin Kidd: The End of the Union?

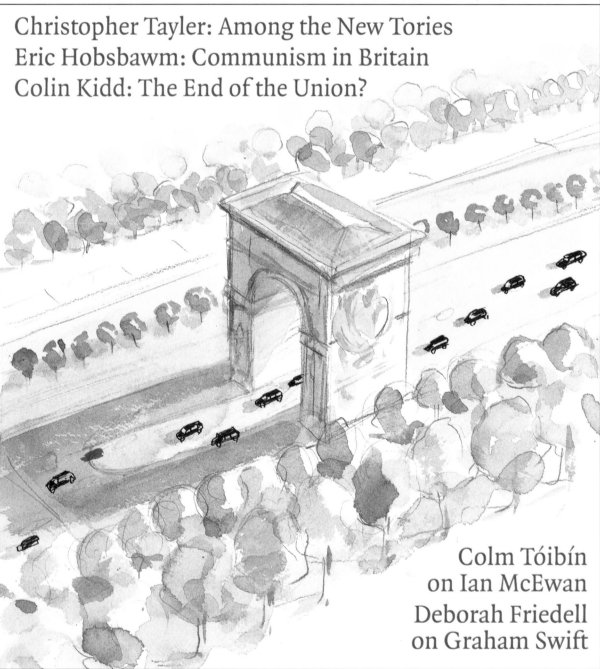

Colm Tóibín
on Ian McEwan
Deborah Friedell
on Graham Swift

Perry Anderson: Italy's Decline

London Review
OF BOOKS

VOLUME 31 NUMBER 4   26 FEBRUARY 2009   £3.20 US & CANADA $4.95

Michael Wood:
The Part about Bolaño

Eric Hobsbawm:
Mandarin Science

Gilberto Perez:
Time and Tarkovsky

Amira Hass:
After Gaza

Steve Fraser:
Emma Goldman

David Kaiser:
Paul Dirac

Reflections on the Present Crisis

London Review
OF BOOKS

VOLUME 23 NUMBER 19   4 OCTOBER 2001   £2.95 US & CANADA $3.95

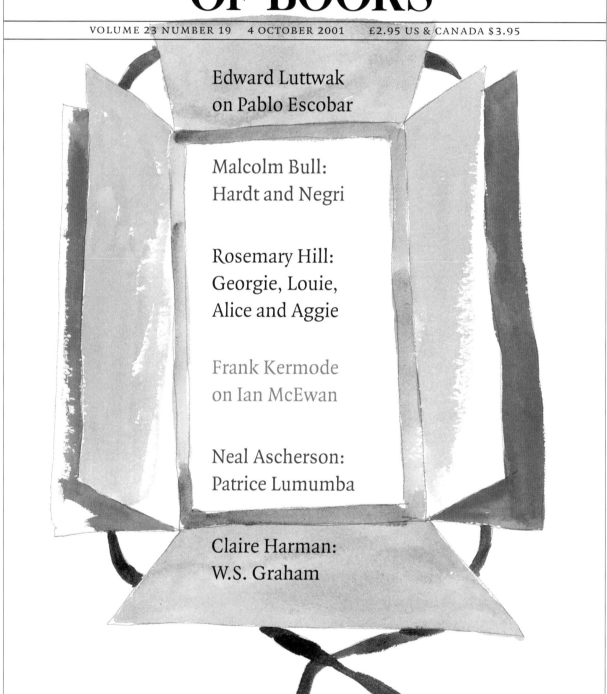

Tony Judt: Bush's Useful Idiots

London Review
OF BOOKS

VOLUME 28 NUMBER 18   21 SEPTEMBER 2006   £2.99 US & CANADA $3.95

John Sutherland: The Great Melanie Phillips Disaster

London Review
OF BOOKS

VOLUME 18 NUMBER 19   3 OCTOBER 1996   £2.25 US & CANADA $2.95

Thomas Lynch:
My Favourite Hypochondriac

James Wood on God

Richard Poirier:
Melville's Pursuit
of Failure

Tom Nairn
on Pol Pot

Thomas Lynch: An Undertaker's Story

London Review
OF BOOKS

VOLUME 16 NUMBER 24   22 DECEMBER 1994   £2.15 US & CANADA $2.95

Adam Phillips: Who can
tell us what we want?

Frank Kermode on
Harold Bloom's Canon

Iain Sinclair goes downriver
with P.D. James

Hilary Mantel on Doris Lessing

Edward Luttwak: America's
New Four-Party System

Adam Phillips on Mourning

London Review
OF BOOKS

VOLUME 21 NUMBER 4   18 FEBRUARY 1999   £2.70 US & CANADA $3.95

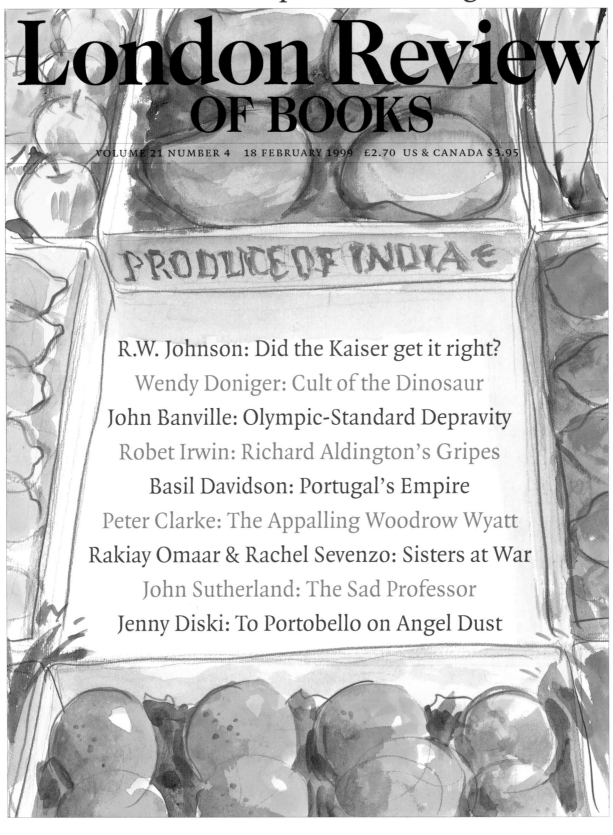

E.J. Hobsbawm on Duke Ellington

London Review
OF BOOKS

VOLUME 16 NUMBER 22   24 NOVEMBER 1994   £2.15 US & CANADA $2.95

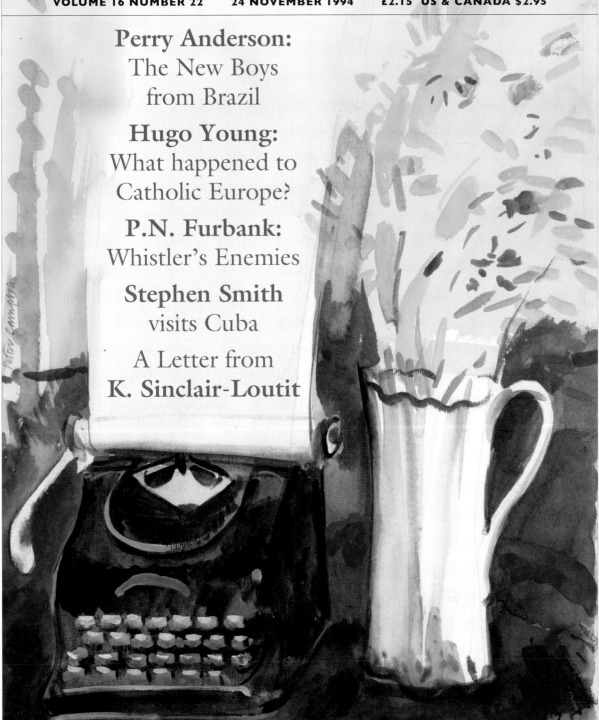

IAIN SINCLAIR wants a Boris Bike

London Review
OF BOOKS

VOLUME 33 NUMBER 2 · 20 JANUARY 2011 · £3.20 US & CANADA $4.95

SLAVOJ ŽIŽEK: Gentlemen of the Left

TARIQ ALI: 'Hello, Mr Yankee Go Home'

MAHMOOD MAMDANI: Congo Explained

SEAMUS PERRY on Tennyson

Condoleezza Rice says her prayers

Pankaj Mishra: Exporting Democracy

London Review
OF BOOKS

VOLUME 30 NUMBER 4   21 FEBRUARY 2008   £3.20 US & CANADA $4.95

Stephen Burt on Robert Creeley

Bernard Porter: Torching the
White House

A.N. Wilson: Was Shaw gay?

London Review
OF BOOKS

VOLUME 18 NUMBER 12   20 JUNE 1996   £2.25 US & CANADA $2.95

Richard Rorty bins sin

Adam Phillips: 'On Interest'

James Wood addresses Seamus Heaney

Ian Hamilton on Ford Madox Ford's
Art-Worship, Editorial Acumen and Messy Life

Jacqueline Rose on Virginia Woolf

London Review
OF BOOKS

VOLUME 19 NUMBER 2   23 JANUARY 1997   £2.25 US & CANADA $2.95

R.W. Johnson: The True Importance of Enoch Powell

Ruth Padel: Piangi, piangi, o misera

Donald MacKenzie: Disinventing Nuclear Weapons

James Davidson: Indigestion in Ancient Times

Iain Sinclair:
Transporting Beneficial Herbs

Ian Gilmour on the Tory Leadership

London Review
OF BOOKS

VOLUME 27 NUMBER 20   20 OCTOBER 2005   £2.99 US & CANADA $3.95

Eric Hobsbawm: Budapest 1956

London Review
OF BOOKS

VOLUME 28 NUMBER 22   16 NOVEMBER 2006   £2.99 US & CANADA $4.95

Jeremy Harding meets Elias Khoury
Frank Kermode remembers William Empson

Ferdinand Mount: The Postponement Years
R.W. Johnson: Thatcher's Boy
Michael Hofmann: The Strangeness of Robert Walser

JAMES MEEK: The NHS Goes Private

London Review
OF BOOKS

VOLUME 33 NUMBER 18   22 SEPTEMBER 2011   £3.20 US & CANADA $4.95

RORY STEWART reports from Tripoli
JENNY DISKI: Which one of you is Jesus?
MICHAEL WOOD on Julian Barnes
SADAKAT KADRI: Bench Rage

Edward Luttwak: Death by Capitalism

London Review
OF BOOKS

VOLUME 20 NUMBER 18   17 SEPTEMBER 1998   £2.50   US & CANADA $2.95

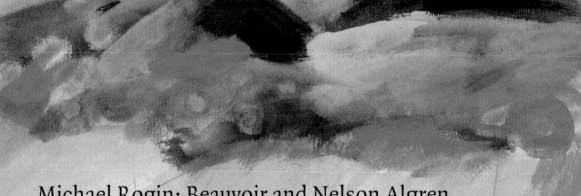

Michael Rogin: Beauvoir and Nelson Algren
C.K. Stead: Poem for Les Murray
Timothy Garton Ash: '48, '68, '89
V.G. Kiernan: Memories of the CP
Peter Campbell: Pretty Rothko
Denise Riley: Naming the Canvas
Peter Wollen: Godard turns over
Armand Marie Leroi: Social Selection
Brian Rotman: Solace in Numbers
D.J. Enright: Suffolk Blues
Elaine Showalter: Isaac Bashevis Singer
Lorna Scott Fox: Mario Vargas Llosa
John Sutherland: David Storey
Richard Gott: Victor Jara's Chile
J. Hoberman: Popular (Front)Songs

Alan Bennett: 'Nights in the Gardens of Spain'

London Review
OF BOOKS

VOLUME 20 NUMBER 19   1 OCTOBER 1998   £2.50   US & CANADA $2.95

Jeremy Harding: Benjamin's Last Day

London Review
OF BOOKS

VOLUME 29 NUMBER 14   19 JULY 2007   £2.99 US & CANADA $4.95

Alan Bennett: 'The Uncommon Reader'

London Review
OF BOOKS

VOLUME 29 NUMBER 5   8 MARCH 2007   £2.99 US & CANADA $4.95

T.J. Clark: A Savonarolan Bonfire

London Review
OF BOOKS

VOLUME 27 NUMBER 18   22 SEPTEMBER 2005   £2.99 US & CANADA $3.95

Eric Hobsbawm: The Central Event of the 20th Century

London Review
OF BOOKS

VOLUME 18 NUMBER 21   31 OCTOBER 1996   £2.25 US & CANADA $2.95

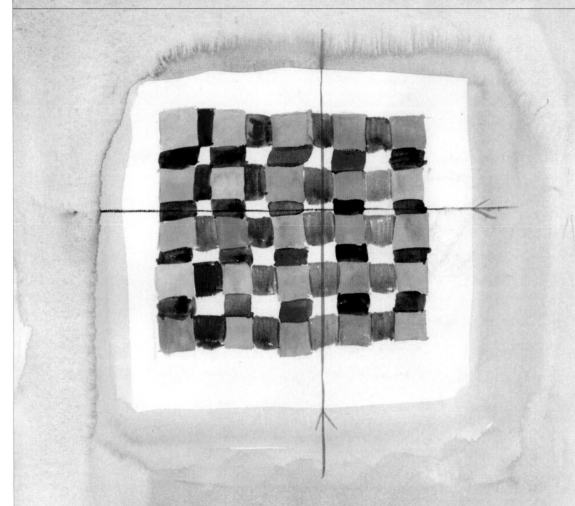

Paul Foot: What Scott Won't Say

London Review
OF BOOKS

VOLUME 16 NUMBER 3   10 FEBRUARY 1994   £2.10 US & CANADA $2.95

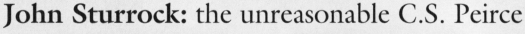
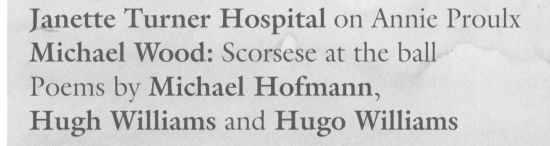

Peter Clarke: Young Margaret

London Review
OF BOOKS

VOLUME 17 NUMBER 13   6 JULY 1995   £2.15 US & CANADA $2.95

Nicholas Spice: The Case against Public Music

Simon Kelner: Murdoch Strikes Again!

Frank Kermode on William Golding

Andrew O'Hagan: Versions of Pastoral

London Review
OF BOOKS

VOLUME 23 NUMBER 6   22 MARCH 2001   £2.95 US & CANADA $3.95

'We are responsible for keeping the landscape the way
people say they are proud to have it – but who pays for it?
The people down the road selling postcards of
the Lake District are making much more than the
farmers who keep the land so photogenic.'

Will Cockbain, hill farmer

Jim Holt: It's the Oil, Stupid

London Review
OF BOOKS

VOLUME 29 NUMBER 20   18 OCTOBER 2007   £3.20 US & CANADA $4.95

Iain Sinclair: The Razing of East London

London Review
OF BOOKS

VOLUME 30 NUMBER 12   19 JUNE 2008   £3.20 US & CANADA $4.95

Thomas Jones: The Last Days of eBay

James Davidson: Atlantis at Last!

Patrick Cockburn: A New Deal for Iraq

Keith Gessen: A Sad Old Literary Man

Ian Gilmour remembers the Profumo Case

London Review
OF BOOKS

VOLUME 28 NUMBER 20   19 OCTOBER 2006   £2.99 US & CANADA $3.95

Terry Eagleton: The Otherness Business

London Review
OF BOOKS

VOLUME 23 NUMBER 16   23 AUGUST 2001   £2.95 US & CANADA $3.95

Keith Gessen: Khodorkovsky's Rise and Fall

London Review
OF BOOKS

VOLUME 32 NUMBER 4   25 FEBRUARY 2010   £3.20 US & CANADA $4.95

Christmas Books

London Review
OF BOOKS

VOLUME 16 NUMBER 23   8 DECEMBER 1994   £2.15 US & CANADA $2.95

Nick Laird: A Week in Mid-Ulster

London Review
OF BOOKS

VOLUME 27 NUMBER 9   5 MAY 2005   £2.99 US & CANADA $3.95

Slavoj Žižek: Improve Your Performance!

London Review
OF BOOKS

VOLUME 25 NUMBER 10   22 MAY 2003   £2.95 US & CANADA $3.95

Adam Phillips:
'Paranoid
Modernism'

Jenny Diski:
In the Vilna
Ghetto

Donald MacKenzie:
Ethnoaccountancy

Michael Hofmann:
The Charm of
Hugo Williams

Leofranc
Holford-Strevens:
Do you speak
Punic?

R.W. Johnson:
All about Eden

Poems by
Robert Pinsky,
Raymond Friel
and Tony Harrison

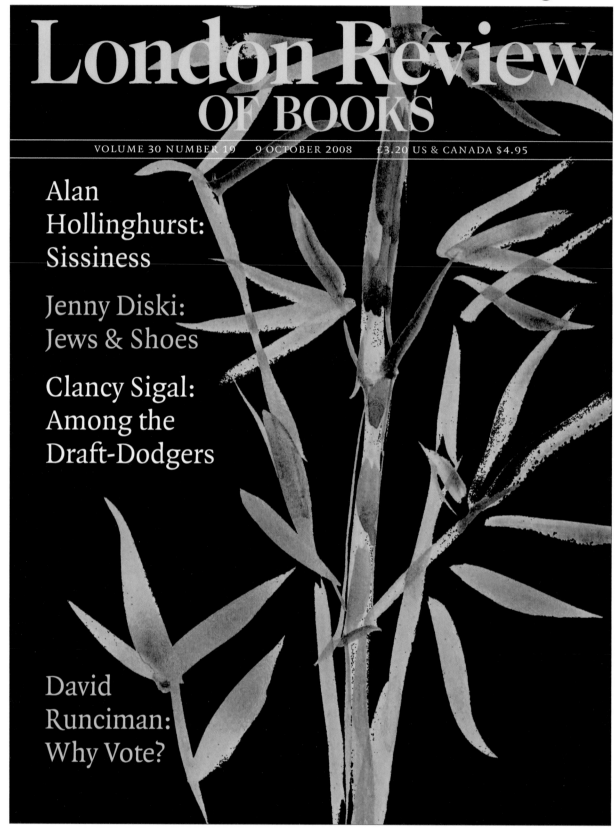

Jonathan Raban: Sarah Palin's Cunning

London Review
OF BOOKS

VOLUME 30 NUMBER 19   9 OCTOBER 2008   £3.20 US & CANADA $4.95

Alan
Hollinghurst:
Sissiness

Jenny Diski:
Jews & Shoes

Clancy Sigal:
Among the
Draft-Dodgers

David
Runciman:
Why Vote?

Bruce Ackerman: The Supreme Court under Threat

London Review
OF BOOKS

VOLUME 27 NUMBER 4   17 FEBRUARY 2005   £2.99 US & CANADA $3.95

Andrew O'Hagan: Robert Louis Stevenson
Brian Rotman: Why did the eternal one arrive so late?
Marina Warner: Girls Are Rubbish
J. Hoberman: The Strangest Personality Ever to Lead the Free World

Frank Kermode thinks about money

London Review
OF BOOKS

VOLUME 19 NUMBER 18   18 SEPTEMBER 1997   £2.25 US & CANADA $2.95

Tom Nairn: The Empire's Last Stand

London Review
OF BOOKS

VOLUME 26 NUMBER 12   24 JUNE 2004   £2.95 US & CANADA $3.95

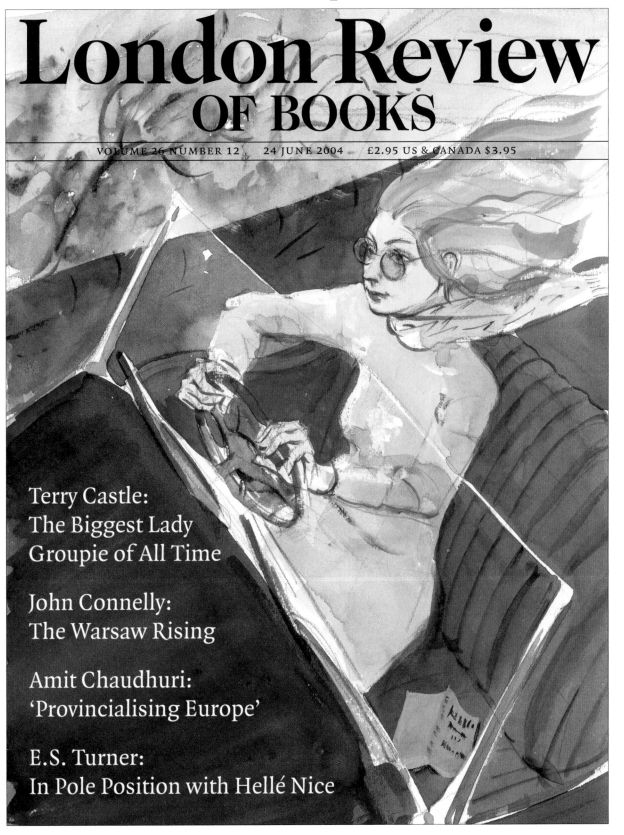

Terry Castle:
The Biggest Lady
Groupie of All Time

John Connelly:
The Warsaw Rising

Amit Chaudhuri:
'Provincialising Europe'

E.S. Turner:
In Pole Position with Hellé Nice

Frank Kermode: The Shudder

London Review
OF BOOKS

VOLUME 32 NUMBER 9   13 MAY 2010   £3.20 US & CANADA $4.95

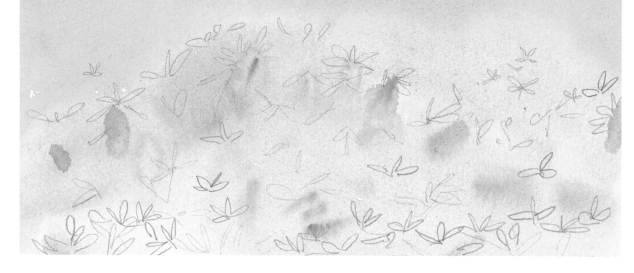

Jeremy Harding: When the Food Runs Out

Gareth Peirce: The Case against Extradition

David Bromwich: The Establishment President

John Barrell celebrates topography

Alan Bennett: A Cure for Arthritis

London Review
OF BOOKS

VOLUME 22 NUMBER 21   2 NOVEMBER 2000   £2.75 US & CANADA $3.95

The Corruption of Literary Biography:
Richard Poirier on Atlas's Bellow
John Barrell on Holmes's Coleridge

James Davidson: Face to Face with Merce Cunningham

Paul Foot: The Government's Favourite Accountants

Jerry Fodor: Where does Tosca get the bread knife from?

Lorna Scott Fox: Haunted by du Maurier

Jeremy Harding: The End of Jihad

London Review
OF BOOKS

VOLUME 24 NUMBER 14   25 JULY 2002   £2.95 US & CANADA $3.95

Michael Byers:
Against Pre-Emption

Robert
Crawford on
the Radical
Burns

Slavoj Žižek:
Lenin's Breakthrough

Jenny Diski
on Catherine M.

John Upton:
Ezekiel in
Custody

Alan Bennett: 'Two in Torquay'

London Review
OF BOOKS

VOLUME 25 NUMBER 13   10 JULY 2003   £2.99 US & CANADA $3.95

David Runciman: What are referendums for?

James Davidson pays tribute to the Persians

Anne Barton: Variations on Elizabeth I

John Lanchester: Unbelievable Blair

Nicholas Penny: Manet/Velázquez

Blair Worden: A Play for Plotters

Ross McKibbin: Origins of the Present Mess

London Review
OF BOOKS

VOLUME 25 NUMBER 15   7 AUGUST 2003   £2.99 US & CANADA $3.95

London Review
OF BOOKS

VOLUME 23 NUMBER 13   5 JULY 2001   £2.95 US & CANADA $3.95

HUGH ROBERTS: Who said Gaddafi had to go?

London Review
OF BOOKS

VOLUME 33 NUMBER 22   17 NOVEMBER 2011   £3.20 US & CANADA $4.95

Other Artwork

Mourjou, Auvergne

The Campbells' Kitchen

Kapiti Island,
New Zealand

Figeac, Lot

Cover, LRB Diary

v: 20ʲ June Many happy returns: P.

Self-Portrait

Patchwork version of an LRB cover given to Peter Campbell by Bryony Dalefield for his 60th birthday

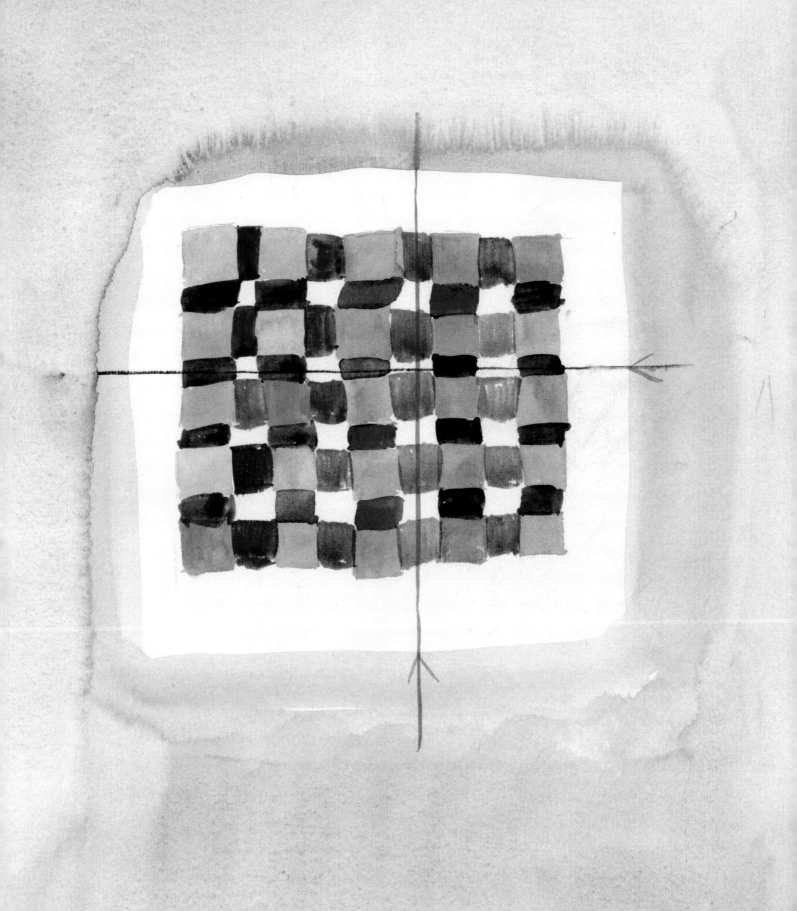

Postcards made for friends

A local nymph delivers rain to Umbria

NO1 BEDROOM, PLACE DE L'EGLISE MOURJOU

CRIME

BIOGRAPHY

BIOGRAPHY

PHILOSOPHY

DRAMA

FILM

Natural History

149

Invitations to subscribe

Looking forward to some time on your own?
Subscribe

Bored with your partner's conversation?
Subscribe

Through with the world? Revive your faith in the life of the mind with a subscription to the London Review of Books.

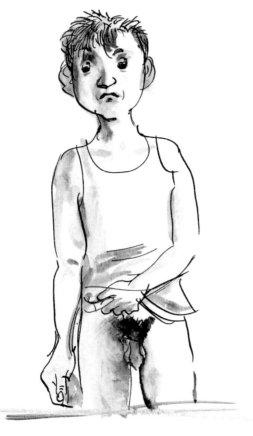

Be Bold
Subscribe

Reach the heights
Subscribe

Get fell in
Subscribe

Aimez-vous les sensations fortes?
Subscribe to the London Review of Books.

Astonish your public
Subscribe

TIME RUNNING OUT

HAS EXPIRED

The gift which begins when the party's over

The gift which begins when the party's over

Don't imbibe
Subscribe

It is written
Subscribe

If the dog you send out for the paper
doesn't come back to hell with him
Subscribe

Don't drift
Subscribe

Blocked?
Subscribe

Do it the easy way
Subscribe

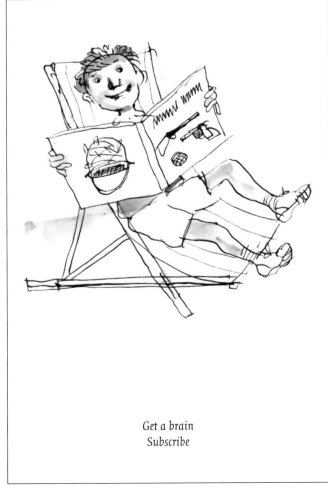

Get a brain
Subscribe

Treat yourself
Subscribe

Books

New Zealand School Publications, 1959

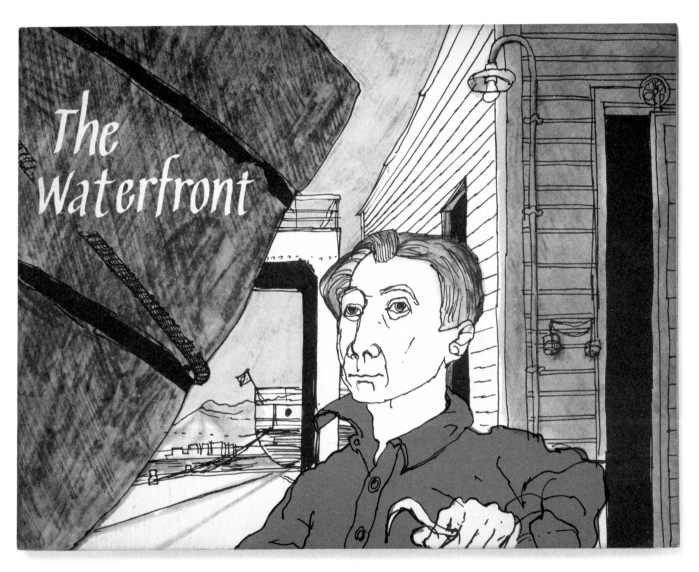

New Zealand School Publications, 1960

Methuen, 1969

Methuen, 1972

BBC, 1969

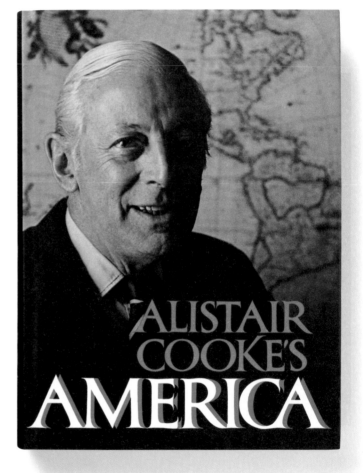

BBC, 1972

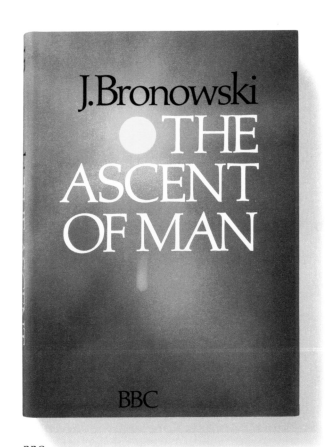

BBC, 1973

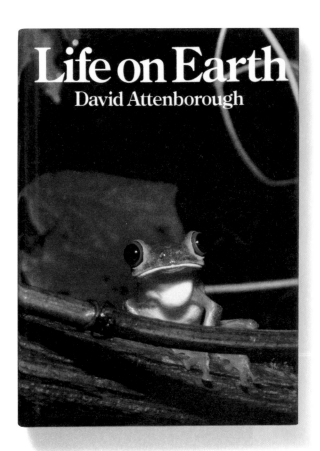

BBC, 1979

A

B

C

[60]

[61]

MASTER

Making
Furniture
from
Paintings

PIECES

Twenty original designs and complete
working instructions for recreating furniture
that appears in masterpieces of world art

Richard Ball & Peter Campbell

Hearst, 1983

MA
MA
FRC

Her
proj
of sl
inst
proj
mat
conv
for
of th
furr

N
exp
usir
furr
ass
furr
ask
furr
fam
as F
The
con
the
crat
inte
stag
ma
anc
res
pre
cre
rev
at v

Go
Re
day
to
sid
a st
mil
fur
mi
int
jux
pai
thr
a li
an
th
bla
ab
dra

Vincent's Chair
by Patrick Daw
from *Chair and Pipe* (Dec. 1888 – Jan. 1889) by Vincent van Gogh (1853–90)
National Gallery, London

V

an Gogh's pipe and tobacco pouch lie on an ordinary rush-seated chair, bathed in the yellow light of Provence. This is probably the best-loved of all images of furniture. But the homely country chair has a dark twin in Gauguin's sinister armchair, which Van Gogh painted in red and green, the colors of violence. It was painted at the same time and speaks of breakdown, departure and death.

Both chairs are empty, and empty chairs were a potent negative symbol to Van Gogh. He admired Luke Fildes's engraving of the empty chair in Charles Dickens's study after the writer's death, and he admits to crying like a child at the sight of his own father's empty chair at the end of a visit to Amsterdam in 1878.

Van Gogh arrived in Arles in February 1888 after two miserable years in Paris. He was in poor health, in need of friendship, but full of hope. He wrote enthusiastically to his devoted brother Theo of the "heavenly blues and yellows" of Arles, its dazzling sunflowers and fresh sky. He rented rooms in the Yellow House on the Place Lamartine near the railway station, and the letters joyfully describe the pleasures of furnishing his new home. He chose a dozen chairs and bought two beds. The second was for Gauguin.

Van Gogh dreamed of founding a school of the south, a community of artists in Arles, and he persuaded Gauguin to occupy the room he so carefully prepared for him in October. The two soon quarreled, and Gauguin decided he must leave. The result was Vincent's first major breakdown, which reached a climax on Christmas Eve. *Le Forum républicain* of December 30th reports: "At 11.30pm last Sunday Vincent Vangogh, a painter born in Holland, arrived at House of Tolerance (brothel) number 1, asked for a certain Rachel and offered her – his ear, saying 'Keep this and treasure it'. Then he left. Told of this action, which could only be that of a poor madman, the police went to his address the next morning and found him in bed and giving barely

15

173

Ben Hartley

Sansom & Co, 2001

27. Bath and Breakfast

56 × 71 cm
Private Collection

Ben's eye was often caught by the untidiness of country life: the back yards of farmhouses full of abandoned machinery and old furniture. On Tod Moor, just above Ermington, he found a bath in a field; from this he managed to create one of his loveliest images. With the subtle brilliance of the colours he begins to match Bonnard, his revered master. The Heineken green of the lager can and the few brown leaves that have found their way onto the window ledge are beautiful touches; so much affection allied to so much technique.

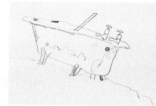

Hayward Gallery with Lund Humphries, 2001

Hayward Gallery and the University of California Press, 1998

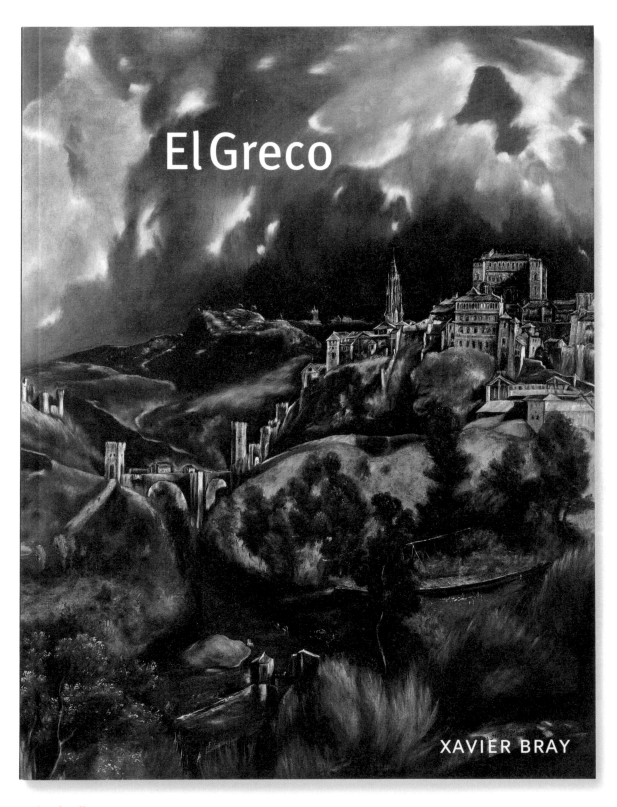

National Gallery, 2004

PAUL KLEE THE NATURE OF CREATION

Hayward Gallery with Lund Humphries, 2002

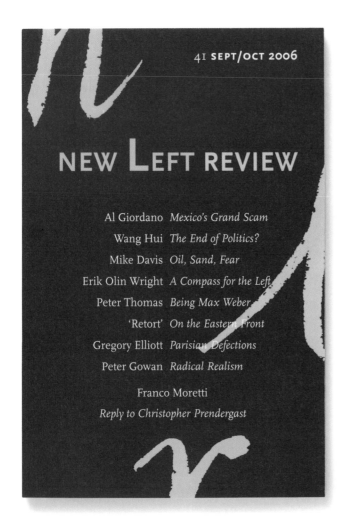

41 SEPT/OCT 2006

NEW LEFT REVIEW

Al Giordano · *Mexico's Grand Scam*

Wang Hui · *The End of Politics?*

Mike Davis · *Oil, Sand, Fear*

Erik Olin Wright · *A Compass for the Left*

Peter Thomas · *Being Max Weber*

'Retort' · *On the Eastern Front*

Gregory Elliott · *Parisian Defections*

Peter Gowan · *Radical Realism*

Franco Moretti

Reply to Christopher Prendergast

57 MAY/JUNE 2009

NEW LEFT REVIEW

Perry Anderson · *Land of Ideas?*

Slavoj Žižek · *Class and Commons*

Roberto Schwarz · *Staging the Crash*

Alain Supiot · *Possible Europes*

Immanuel Wallerstein · *Reflections on Fanon*

Alexander Zevin · *Reordering 68*

Chin-tao Wu · *Biennials Sans Frontières*

Tom Hazeldine · *England's Revolution*

R. Taggart Murphy · *Beyond Bubblenomics*

Leo Panitch & Martijn Konings

Myths of Neoliberal Deregulation

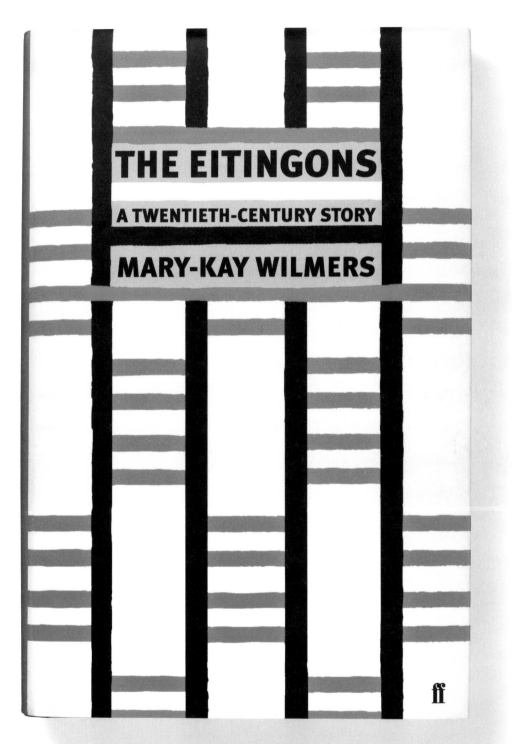

THE EITINGONS

A TWENTIETH-CENTURY STORY

MARY-KAY WILMERS

Faber, 2009

Alan Bennett

THE
CLOTHES
THEY
STOOD
UP IN

A STORY

Profile, 1998

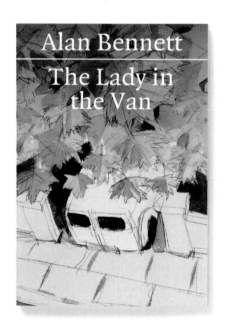

Alan Bennett

The Lady in
the Van

Profile, 1999

Alan Bennett

FATHER!
FATHER!
BURNING
BRIGHT

a story

Profile, 2000

Alan Bennett

THE UNCOMMON READER

Profile, 2008

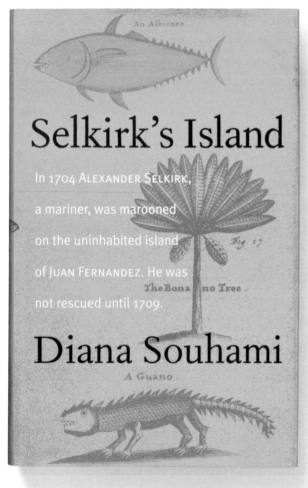

Weidenfeld & Nicolson, 2001

Weidenfeld & Nicolson, 2007

Quentin Blake
La Vie de la Page

Gallimard Jeunesse

Gallimard, 1995

At Low Magnification
Peter Campbell

At LUNCH in France last week, with an expert on cheese and its management, the conversation turned to mites. The four teenage girls who were of the party wanted to know what they were getting their teeth into. Cheese mites are too small to be seen easily with the naked eye. Was there a magnifying glass around? There I could help, I had two of the kind of hand lenses botanists and geologists use in the field. One magnifies by 10, the other by 20. The mites, glistening white blobs, could be seen moving slowly across the grey crust. I hope, but do not expect, to have recruited at least one of the girls to the pleasures of low magnification.

Since I was a child I have hankered after optical instruments. The first was a 5x magnifying glass; the second, a 10x, I used when I briefly studied geology. There have been many others: the telescope (8x) my father bought me when he was on a trip to America; the two pairs of binoculars (7x); the dissecting stereomicroscope (a present to myself), which zooms from around 10x to 40x: the sort of instrument used for inspecting circuit boards, or by palaeontologists when they pick away the matrix to reveal an embedded fossil. I also have an ordinary microscope (a medical school discard) with various objectives and eyepieces, giving much higher magnifications. But playing with that taught me that high magnification goes along with other disciplines: embedding and staining specimens, cutting thin sections, learning to interpret the slices as sections of three-dimensional objects. Those tools of the pathology and biology laboratories were not what I needed.

What really pleases me is the degree of enlargement that takes one not far beyond what the naked eye can see and brings closer and makes sharper the plumage of a distant bird, the detail of a boss or a high stained-glass window in a cathedral, the name of a ship, the structure of insects and plants. Although I have a terrestrial telescope (30x, good for watching birds in estuaries), I have no interest in getting an astronomical one. Still, I'm pleased when someone who has one shows me the rings of Saturn or the mountains of the Moon and I was carried away by Richard Holmes's account in *The Age of Wonder* of the heroic campaigns of observation and telescope-making carried out by Herschel and his sister. In the 1950s I was gripped by descriptions of the casting and polishing of the 200-inch mirror of the Hale telescope on Mount Palomar, and more recently I followed the drama of the error in the configuration of the Hubble telescope mirror and its correction, but by and large I am happy to enjoy the far reaches of magnification in the images the great telescopes produce of exploding stars and clusters of galaxies. I feel the same about huge enlargements of things that are very small. The visual texture of electron microscope images of insects and pollen grains has so much in common with computer-graphic renderings that they read as abstractions.

My optical toys, on the other hand, let you explore what you see, not see something beyond what you know. They enlarge no more than a few times, at the most a few tens of times. Sitting in an orchard last week I saw pied flycatchers make quick excursions from the branches of an apple tree. Without binoculars I wouldn't have been sure that was what they were: to keep track of their progress as they dodged among the tangle of twigs and leaves, a wide, bright view was more important than a highly magnified one. Tremor degrades the image in all hand-held devices, which is why telescopes are used with tripods. In the low-magnification world, as the lens brings the leaf in your hand or the bird in the bush closer, the content of the visible world is multiplied.

Looking at things closely leads to wondering what they are called. The sporadic self-education in natural history that goes with picking up pretty pebbles, shells and plants on country walks, and noticing the fauna, sometimes calls for my kind of optics. We are not like the old ornithologists who made their identifications from dead specimens. (Would Audubon's marvellous, stiffly heraldic illustrations of American birds have looked different if he had had modern binoculars to supplement the work of his shotgun?) The identification of plants sometimes requires more than the evidence of the unaided eye, which has trouble determining degrees and kinds of hairiness, for example: something you need to see if you are after the identity of a grass plant. Rocks, too, will read better enlarged, should you want, say, to identify the minerals that give granite its speckled look.

The Claude glass, the dark, slightly convex mirror that eighteenth- and nineteenth-century tourists and sketchers used to give nature an artistic appearance, reduces a view into something simpler. It is a step towards painting or drawing; and like painting and drawing, it edits detail out. My pleasure comes from finding more than the unaided eye can see, not less, from looking at a bit of a plant and finding an aphid making its ponderous way from behind a leaf or inspecting a dead lavender flower and finding globules of scented oil among faded petals.

First published in the *London Review of Books*,
(Vol. 32 No. 17, 9 September 2010)